Raspberry Pi Robotic Projects

Third Edition

Work through a mix of amazing robotic projects using the Raspberry Pi Zero or the Raspberry Pi 3

Richard Grimmett

BIRMINGHAM - MUMBAI

Raspberry Pi Robotic Projects

Third Edition

First published: February 2014

Second edition: April 2015

Third edition: October 2016

Production reference: 1041016

Published by Packt Publishing Ltd.
Livery Place
35 Livery Street
Birmingham
B3 2PB, UK.

ISBN 978-1-78646-796-6

www.packtpub.com

Credits

Author

Richard Grimmett

Reviewer

Jon Witts

Commissioning Editor

Kartikey Pandey

Acquisition Editor

Tushar Gupta

Content Development Editor

Merint Mathew

Technical Editor

Hussain Kanchwala

Copy Editor

Safis Editing

Project Coordinator

Suzanne Coutinho

Proofreader

Safis Editing

Indexer

Rekha Nair

Graphics

Abhinash Sahu

Production Coordinator

Shraddha Falebhai

About the Author

Richard Grimmett has always been fascinated by computers and electronics from his very first programming project that used Fortran on punch cards. He has a bachelor's and master's degree in electrical engineering and a PhD in leadership studies. He also has 26 years of experience in the Radar and Telecommunications industries and even has one of the original brick phones. Currently, he teaches computer science and electrical engineering at Brigham Young University, Idaho, where his office is filled with many of his robotics projects.

This book is the result of working with many of the wonderful students at BYU-Idaho. It also wouldn't be possible without the help of my wonderful wife, Jeanne.

About the Reviewer

Jon Witts has been working in the IT industry since 2002, specifically in educational IT since 2004. He was introduced to Linux back in 2001 through his collaboration with two German artists who were visiting the arts organisation he was then working with. Having studied fine arts and educational technology, he sought to innovate with open and accessible digital technologies within his creative practice and is happiest when deconstructing technology and finding its limits.

Jon has embedded the use of Raspberry Pi computers in his school as an integral part of the delivery of the computer science curriculum, as well as to run various school clubs and projects. Jon is a Raspberry Pi Certified Educator and also helps to organize and run the Hull Raspberry Jam events.

I would like to thank my wife, Sally, and our three daughters for putting up with all the cables and components around the house, and not least for being so tolerant of the need to dodge the robots racing around the kitchen floor!

www.PacktPub.com

For support files and downloads related to your book, please visit www.PacktPub.com.

Did you know that Packt offers eBook versions of every book published, with PDF and ePub files available? You can upgrade to the eBook version at www.PacktPub.com and as a print book customer, you are entitled to a discount on the eBook copy. Get in touch with us at service@packtpub.com for more details.

At www.PacktPub.com, you can also read a collection of free technical articles, sign up for a range of free newsletters and receive exclusive discounts and offers on Packt books and eBooks.

https://www.packtpub.com/mapt

Get the most in-demand software skills with Mapt. Mapt gives you full access to all Packt books and video courses, as well as industry-leading tools to help you plan your personal development and advance your career.

Why subscribe?

- Fully searchable across every book published by Packt
- Copy and paste, print, and bookmark content
- On demand and accessible via a web browser

Table of Contents

Preface

With the introduction of the Raspberry Pi just a few short years ago, a whole new world of do-it-yourself projects have come to life. This inexpensive but powerful processor provides a wide range of possibilities. When married with third-party hardware and free open source software, the opportunities are endless.

This book provides a step-by-step guide to at least some of these projects. Each chapter will introduce you to a new and different type of project. Each project will have very specific challenges and opportunities to learn new and cool ways to use the Raspberry Pi. Now, these chapters are really just an introduction to the topic; each of these projects would take an entire book to cover all the different aspects.

The book will hopefully inspire you to take the many different skills you have learned and mix and match them into entirely different projects with new and creative capabilities. Explore, for that is the overall theme of this book and of the Raspberry Pi.

What this book covers

Chapter 1, *Getting Started with the Raspberry Pi*, covers the details of setting up a useful development environment on the Raspberry Pi. The chapter begins with a discussion on how to connect power and continues through setting up a full system that is configured and ready to begin connecting any of the amazing devices and software capabilities to develop advanced robotics applications.

Chapter 2, *Building Your Own Futuristic Robot*, talks about the amazing things you can do with the Raspberry Pi, such as control a wheeled robot. This chapter will show you how to add a motor control so you can build your very own autonomous mobile robot. Additionally, one of the amazing features of today's computer system is the ability to input commands and provide output without a screen or keyboard. A few years ago, the concept of a computer that can talk and listen was science fiction, but today it is becoming a standard part of new cell phones. You'll take a standard toy R2D2 and turn it into a responsive robot.

Chapter 3, *Building a Wall-E Robot*, talks about another impressive robotic project, which is a robot modeled after Wall-E—a robot with a tracked base and articulating arms. Servos can be controlled using the Raspberry Pi and some additional USB-controlled hardware. Our robot will also use a Microsoft Kinect to not only have vision but depth perception as well.

Chapter 4, *Building a Robotic Fish*, shows you how to build your very own robot that can swim and show you the world under the water—wouldn't a swimming robot be cool?

Chapter 5, *Creating a Robotic Hand with the Raspberry Pi*, talks about how you have a full toolkit of possibilities now, and how you can use them to build and control a robotic hand that can see and respond to the world around it. In this case, you'll program your hand to follow the movements of your hand using a webcam.

Chapter 6, *A Self-Balancing Robot*, discusses the many recent robotic toys that were built on the concept of self-balancing two-wheeled platform. This chapter shows you how to build a robot that can balance and move using only two wheels.

Chapter 7, *Adding the Raspberry Pi to a Quadcopter*, introduces you to the concept of building a robot that can fly. A robot that can walk, talk, or move is cool, but one that can fly is the ultimate.

Who this book is for

This book is for hobbyists and programmers who are excited about using the Raspberry Pi 3 and Raspberry Pi Zero. It is for those who are taking their first steps towards using these devices to control hardware and software and write simple programs that enable amazing projects. No programming experience is required, just a little computer and mechanical aptitude and the desire to build some interesting projects.

What you need for this book

To download the requisite software list, please refer to the following links: `https://www.packtpub.com/sites/default/files/downloads/RaspberryPiRoboticProjectsSoftwareList.pdf`

Conventions

In this book, you will find a number of text styles that distinguish between different kinds of information. Here are some examples of these styles and an explanation of their meaning.

Code words in text, database table names, folder names, filenames, file extensions, pathnames, dummy URLs, user input, and Twitter handles are shown as follows: "We can include other contexts through the use of the `include` directive."

A block of code is set as follows:

```
ser = serial.Serial("/dev/ttyACM0", 9600)
setAngle(ser, 0, 90)
setAngle(ser, 1, 90)
setAngle(ser, 2, 90)
time.sleep(1)
```

Any command-line input or output is written as follows:

```
sudo apt-get install libasound2-dev
```

New terms and **important words** are shown in bold. Words that you see on the screen, for example, in menus or dialog boxes, appear in the text like this: "Clicking the **Next** button moves you to the next screen."

Warnings or important notes appear in a box like this.

Tips and tricks appear like this.

Reader feedback

Feedback from our readers is always welcome. Let us know what you think about this book—what you liked or disliked. Reader feedback is important for us as it helps us develop titles that you will really get the most out of.

To send us general feedback, simply e-mail feedback@packtpub.com, and mention the book's title in the subject of your message.

If there is a topic that you have expertise in and you are interested in either writing or contributing to a book, see our author guide at www.packtpub.com/authors.

Customer support

Now that you are the proud owner of a Packt book, we have a number of things to help you to get the most from your purchase.

Downloading the color images of this book

We also provide you with a PDF file that has color images of the screenshots/diagrams used in this book. The color images will help you better understand the changes in the output. You can download this file from `https://www.packtpub.com/sites/default/files/down loads/RaspberryPiRoboticProjectsThirdEdition_ColorImages.pdf`.

Errata

Although we have taken every care to ensure the accuracy of our content, mistakes do happen. If you find a mistake in one of our books—maybe a mistake in the text or the code—we would be grateful if you could report this to us. By doing so, you can save other readers from frustration and help us improve subsequent versions of this book. If you find any errata, please report them by visiting `http://www.packtpub.com/submit-errata`, selecting your book, clicking on the **Errata Submission Form link**, and entering the details of your errata. Once your errata are verified, your submission will be accepted and the errata will be uploaded to our website or added to any list of existing errata under the Errata section of that title.

To view the previously submitted errata, go to `https://www.packtpub.com/books/conten t/support` and enter the name of the book in the search field. The required information will appear under the Errata section.

Piracy

Piracy of copyrighted material on the Internet is an ongoing problem across all media. At Packt, we take the protection of our copyright and licenses very seriously. If you come across any illegal copies of our works in any form on the Internet, please provide us with the location address or website name immediately so that we can pursue a remedy.

Please contact us at `copyright@packtpub.com` with a link to the suspected pirated material.

We appreciate your help in protecting our authors and our ability to bring you valuable content.

Questions

If you have a problem with any aspect of this book, you can contact us at `questions@packtpub.com`, and we will do our best to address the problem.

1

Getting Started with the Raspberry Pi

Welcome to the exciting world of Raspberry Pi! Since its introduction just a few years ago, it has gained a huge following of *Do-It-Yourselfers*, who use the small but versatile processor family to build a wide variety of projects, and for good reason. The entire set of Raspberry Pi offers a range of solid performance at a low cost. With the addition of inexpensive additional hardware and free, open source software, the Raspberry Pi can be used to produce a wide range of projects, including robots that can roll, walk, fly, and swim.

The Raspberry Pi can do amazing things, but first you'll need to understand how to access all of this capability. In this chapter, you'll learn about the following subjects:

- Providing power to the board
- Connecting a display, keyboard, and mouse
- Loading and configuring the operating system
- Configuring the board for remote access

There are several versions of the Raspberry Pi, but there are two versions that you can choose to do the projects in this book. The first is the **Raspberry Pi Zero**, the smallest and least expensive of the Raspberry Pi processor boards. It boasts a Broadcom BCM2835 application processor that features a 1 GHz ARM11 core and 512MB of LPDDR2 SDRAM. The board also has a microSD card slot, a mini HDMI socket for 1080p60 video output, micro USB sockets for data and power, and a 40-pin GPIO header in a small form factor.

The other choice is the Raspberry Pi 3, a slightly larger version, but with higher performance and more hardware connections built right into the board. The Raspberry Pi 3 offers a 1.2 GHz 64-bit quad-core ARM Cortex-A53 CPU (~3 x the performance of the Raspberry Pi Zero). In contrast to the Raspberry Pi Zero, it has a built-in microSD card slot, a standard HDMI socket for 1080p60 video output, a micro USB socket for power, a built-in four-port USB connector, and a 40-pin GPIO header. It also provides Integrated 802.11n wireless LAN and Bluetooth 4.1. If you are not sure which board is right for you, it may make sense to read through this chapter, see how to power up and configure both, and then decide which is right for you.

Setting up the Raspberry Pi 3

The Raspberry Pi 3, with more hardware available as part of the standard product, is similar, but a bit easier to configure, than the Raspberry Pi Zero, since almost all the hardware you need is available right on the Raspberry Pi 3.

Here are the items you'll need to set up the Raspberry Pi 3:

- A Raspberry Pi 3
- A micro USB cable and power supply to provide power to the board
- A display with an HDMI video input
- A keyboard and mouse
- A micro SD card – with at least 4 GB capacity
- A micro SD card writer
- Another computer that is connected to the Internet

Before you get started, let's get familiar with the Raspberry Pi 3. Here is an image of the hardware:

Here are the connections labeled for your information:

One of the first things you'll need to do is provide power for the board.

Powering the board

One of the first issues you'll want to consider is how to power the board. To do this, you need to connect through the USB power connection. There are two choices for providing power to the Raspberry Pi Zero:

1. Connect the micro USB connector labeled power to a 5V DC source powered by a USB power supply. This can be either a power supply that can plug directly into an outlet, or power supplied by a powered USB port such as those available on most computers.

2. Connect the micro USB connector to a battery. The simplest type of connection is to a battery that has a USB connector, like those used to charge cellphones. Here is an image of just such a battery:

In both cases, make sure that the unit can supply enough current. You'll need a supply that can provide at least 1000 mA at 5V. Do not plug in the board just yet; you first need to connect the rest of the hardware and configure the micro SD card. However, you are now ready to connect the rest of the hardware.

Hooking up a keyboard, mouse, and display

The next step is to connect a keyboard, mouse, and display to the Raspberry Pi 3. For the Raspberry Pi 3, this is very straightforward: simply plug the USB connectors of the keyboard and mouse into one of the four USB connectors on the Raspberry Pi 3.

Now, you'll also need a display. There are a number of different video standards; here is an image of some of the most common ones, for reference:

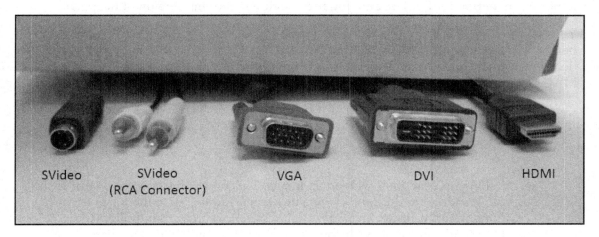

| SVideo | SVideo (RCA Connector) | VGA | DVI | HDMI |

There is an HDMI connector on the Raspberry Pi 3. You can connect directly to an HDMI display using an HDMI cable. If your display has a DVI connector, you can purchase an HDMI to DVI cable.

You are almost ready to plug in the Raspberry Pi 3. Even though your hardware configuration is complete, you'll still need to complete the next section to power on the device. So, let's figure out how to install an operating system.

Installing the operating system

Now that your hardware is ready, you need to download and image an operating system to a microSD card. The Raspberry Pi 3 provides a lot of different choices. You'll stick with Linux, an open source version of Unix, on your Raspberry Pi 3. Linux, unlike Windows, Android, or iOS, is not tightly controlled by a single company. It is a grassroots effort from a wide community, mostly open source and, while it is available for free, it grows and develops a bit more chaotically.

A number of different versions of Linux have emerged, each built on a core set of similar capabilities referred to as the Linux kernel. These core capabilities are all based on the Linux specification. However, they are packaged slightly differently, and developed, supported, and packaged by different organizations. The Raspberry Pi community has become standardized on **Raspbian**, a **Debian** distribution of Linux for the Raspberry Pi. So, you are going to install and run Raspbian on your Raspberry Pi 3.

The newest version of Debian is called **Jessie**, after the cowgirl in Toy Story. This is the naming convention for Debian, and you need to download this version of Raspbian.

You can purchase a card that has Raspbian installed, or you can download it onto your personal computer and then install it on the card. To download a distribution, you need to decide if you are going to use a Windows computer to download and create an SD card, a MAC OS X, or a Linux machine. Here are the steps for Windows and Linux machines:

 For directions on the MAC OS X, go to http://www.raspberrypi.org/do cumentation/installation/installing-images/mac.md.

1. Firstly, you need to download an image. This part of the process is similar for both Windows and Linux. Open a browser window, go to the Raspberry Pi Foundation's website, https://www.raspberrypi.org/, and select the **Downloads** selection at the top of the page. This will give you a variety of download choices. Go to the **Raspbian** section, and select the .zip file just to the right of the image identifier. You need the latest version, but not the lite one. This will download an archived file that has the image for your Raspbian operating system. Note the default username and password; you'll need them later.

2. If you're using Windows, you'll need to unzip the file using an archiving program such as 7-Zip, available at http://www.7-zip.org/. This will leave you with a file that has the .img extension—a file that can be imaged onto your card. Next, you need a program that can write the image to the card. I use *Image Writer* for Windows. You can find a link to this program at the top of the download section on the http://www.raspberrypi.org website.

Plug your card into the PC, run this program, and you should see the following:

3. Select the device card and the image you downloaded earlier; it should look something like the following screenshot:

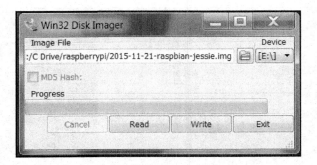

4. Click on the **Write** button. This will take some time, perhaps as long as 15 minutes. When it is complete, exit the program and you'll have your microSD card with the image.

5. If you are using Linux, you need to unarchive the file and then write it to the card. You can do all of this with one command. However, you do need to find the /dev device label for your card. You can do this with the `ls -la /dev/sd*` command. If you run this before you plug in your card, you might see something like the following screenshot:

```
richard@vicki-automated: ~
richard@vicki-automated:~$ ls -la /dev/sd*
brw-rw---- 1 root disk 8, 0 Jul  4 10:34 /dev/sda
brw-rw---- 1 root disk 8, 1 Jul  4 10:34 /dev/sda1
brw-rw---- 1 root disk 8, 2 Jul  4 10:34 /dev/sda2
brw-rw---- 1 root disk 8, 5 Jul  4 10:34 /dev/sda5
richard@vicki-automated:~$
```

6. After plugging in your card, you might see something like the following screenshot:

```
richard@vicki-automated: ~
richard@vicki-automated:~$ ls -la /dev/sd*
brw-rw---- 1 root disk 8,  0 Jul  4 10:34 /dev/sda
brw-rw---- 1 root disk 8,  1 Jul  4 10:34 /dev/sda1
brw-rw---- 1 root disk 8,  2 Jul  4 10:34 /dev/sda2
brw-rw---- 1 root disk 8,  5 Jul  4 10:34 /dev/sda5
brw-rw---- 1 root disk 8, 16 Jul 11 09:50 /dev/sdb
brw-rw---- 1 root disk 8, 17 Jul 11 09:50 /dev/sdb1
brw-rw---- 1 root disk 8, 18 Jul 11 09:50 /dev/sdb2
richard@vicki-automated:~$
```

7. Note that your card is at sdb. Now, go to the directory in which you downloaded the archived image file and use the following command:

    ```
    sudo dd if=2015-11-21-raspbian-jessie.img  of=/dev/sdX
    ```

8. The 2015-11-21-raspbian-jessie.img command will be replaced by the image file that you downloaded and /dev/sdX will be replaced by your card ID, in this example, /dev/sdb. Be careful to specify the correct device, as this can overwrite the data on any of your drives. Also, this may take a few minutes. Once the file is written, eject the card, and you are ready to plug it into the board and apply the power.

Now that you have completed those steps, make sure that your Raspberry Pi 3 is unplugged and install the SD card into the slot. Then power the device. After the device boots, you should get the following screen:

You are up and running!

If you are using a US keyboard, you may need to edit the keyboard file for your keyboard to use nano effectively. To do this, use the drop-down menu in the upper left-hand corner of the screen, choose **Preferences | Mouse and Keyboard Settings**, and then select the **Keyboard** tab. You can then choose the correct keyboard for your configuration.

Now you are ready to start interacting with the system! You can bring up a Terminal window and start typing commands.

Adding Internet access

The Raspberry Pi 3 has a standard LAN connector. To connect the Raspberry Pi 3, simply plug it into an active LAN. The Raspberry Pi also has built-in WLAN capability. If you are going to connect wirelessly, make sure that you have a wireless access point available. You can then use the Raspberry Pi's Wireless LAN manager to connect. To do this, select the LAN manager icon in the upper right-hand corner of the graphical user interface (GUI):

You can then select the network you wish to connect to. Enter your password and you should be connected.

Accessing your Raspberry Pi 3 from your host PC

Once you have established an Internet network connection with your device, you can access it from your host computer. There are three ways to access your system from your remote computer:

1. The first is through a Terminal interface called **SSH**.

2. The second way is by using a program called **VNC server**. This allows you to open a graphical user interface remotely, which mirrors the graphical user interface on the Raspberry Pi 3.

3. Finally, you can transfer files through a program called **WinSCP**, which is custom-made for this purpose. You can use a program called **scp** for Linux.

So firstly, make sure that your basic system is up and working. Open a Terminal window and check the IP address of your unit. You're going to need this, however, you communicate with the system. Do this by using the `ifconfig` command. It should produce what is shown in the following screenshot:

You need `inet addr` to contact your board through the Ethernet. If you are using a wireless device to gain access to the Internet, your wireless router will set the IPv4addr shown in the `wlan0` section of this information. You also need an SSH terminal program running on your remote computer. An SSH terminal is a **Secure Shell (SSH)** connection, which simply means that you'll be able to access your board and give it commands by typing them into your remote computer. The response from the Raspberry Pi 3 will appear in the remote computer's Terminal window.

 If you'd like to know more about SSH, visit `https://www.siteground.co m/tutorials/ssh/`.

If you are running Microsoft Windows, you can download an alternative application. My personal favorite is **PuTTY**. It is free and does a very good job of saving your configuration so that you don't have to type it in every time. Type `putty` in a search engine and you'll soon come to a page that supports a download. Alternatively, you can go to `http://www.putty.org`.

Download PuTTY to your Microsoft Windows machine. Then, run `putty.exe`. You should see a configuration window that looks something like the following screenshot:

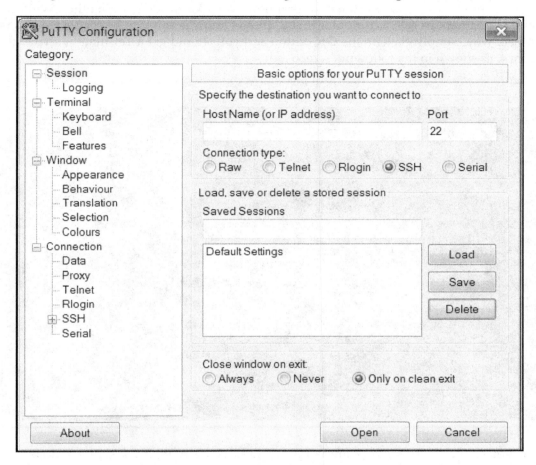

Type the `inet addr` from the previous page in the **Host Name** space and make sure that the **SSH** selection is selected. You may want to save this configuration under Raspberry Pi so that you can reload it each time.

When you click on the **Open** button, the system will try to open a Terminal window onto your Raspberry Pi through the LAN connection. The first time you do this, you will get a warning about an RSA key, as the two computers don't know about each other. Windows therefore, complains that a computer that it doesn't know is about to be connected in a fairly intimate way. Simply click on the **OK** button and you should get a Terminal with a login prompt, as shown in the following screenshot:

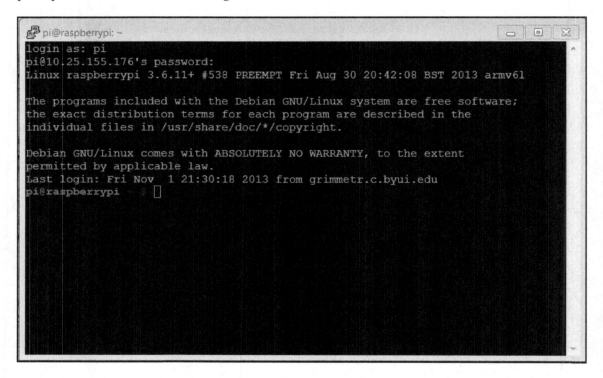

Now you can log in and issue commands to your Raspberry Pi. If you'd like to do this from a Linux machine, the process is even simpler. Bring up a Terminal window and then type `ssh pi@xxx.xxx.xxx.xxx`, where `xxx.xxx.xxx.xxx` is the `inet addr` of your device. This will then bring you to the login screen of your Raspberry Pi, which should look similar to the preceding screenshot.

SSH is a really useful tool to communicate with your Raspberry Pi. However, sometimes you need a graphical look at your system and you don't necessarily want to connect to a display. You can get this on your remote computer by using an application called **vncserver**. You'll need to install a version of this on your Raspberry Pi by typing `sudo apt-get install tightvncserver` in a Terminal window on your Raspberry Pi. This is a perfect opportunity to use SSH, by the way.

Tightvncserver is an application that allows you to view your complete Raspberry Pi. Once you have it installed, you need to start the server by typing `vncserver` in a Terminal window on the Raspberry Pi. You will be prompted for a password and password verification, and then you will be asked if you'd like to have a view-only password. Remember the password that you entered-you'll need it to log in via VNC Viewer remotely.

You need a VNC Viewer application for your remote computer. On my Windows system, I use an application called **RealVNC**. When I start the application, it gives me the following:

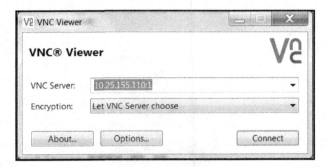

Enter the **VNC Server** address, which is the IP address of your Raspberry Pi, and click on **Connect**. You will see a pop-up window, as shown in the following screenshot:

Type in the password that you just entered while starting vncserver. You should then get a graphical view of your Raspberry Pi that looks like the following screenshot:

You can now access all of the capabilities of your system, although they may be slower if you are doing a graphics-intensive data transfer.

There are ways to make vncserver start automatically on boot. I have not used them; I prefer to type the `vncserver` command from an SSH application when I want the application running. This keeps your running applications to a minimum and, more importantly, presents fewer security risks. If you want to start yours each time you boot, there are several places on the Internet that show you how to configure this. Try the following website:

`http://www.havetheknowhow.com/Configure-the-server/Run-VNC-on-boot.html`

To view this Raspberry Pi desktop from a remote Linux computer running Ubuntu, for example, you can type `sudo apt-get install xtightvncviewer` and then start it by using `xtightvncviewer 10.25.155.110:1` and supplying the chosen password.

Linux has viewers with graphical interfaces such as **Remmina Remote Desktop Client** (select the **VNC-Virtual Network Computing** protocol), which might be used instead of `xtightvncviewer`. Here is a screenshot of the **Remote Desktop Viewer**:

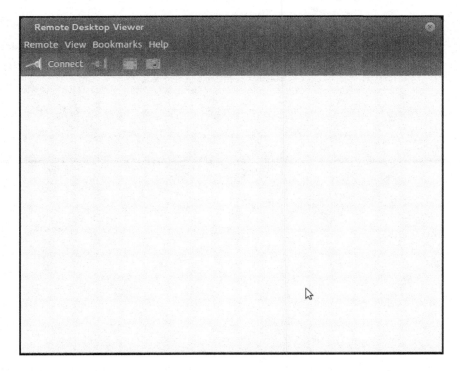

Make sure that vncserver is running on the Raspberry Pi. The easiest way to do this is to log in using SSH and run vncserver at the prompt. Now, click **Connect** on the **Remote Desktop Viewer**. Fill in the screen as follows; in the **Protocol** selection, choose **VNC**, and you should see the following:

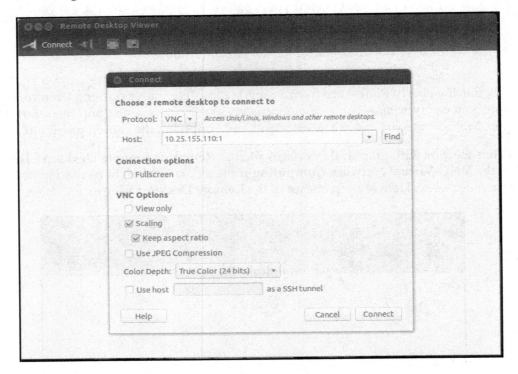

Now, enter the **Host** Internet address, making sure that you include a :1 at the end, and then click on **Connect**. You'll need to enter the vncserver password you set up, as shown in the following screenshot:

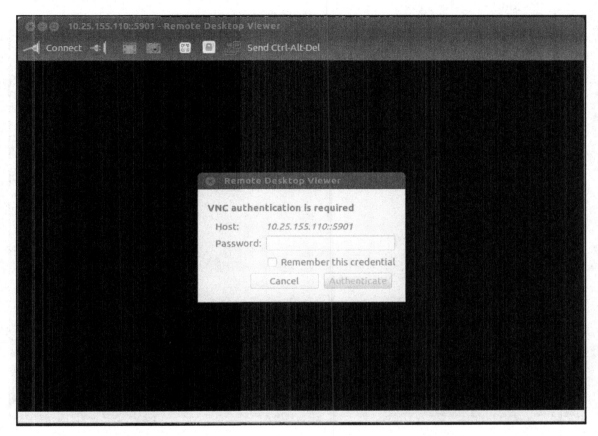

Now you should be able to see the graphical screen of the Raspberry Pi. To access the Raspberry Pi graphically from a Mac or other Apple device, you can still use RealVNC Viewer. See https://www.realvnc.com/products/ for more information.

The final piece of software that I like to use with Windows is a free application called **WinSCP**. To download and install this piece of software, go to `https://winscp.net/` and follow the instructions to download and install. Once installed, run the program. It will open the following dialog box:

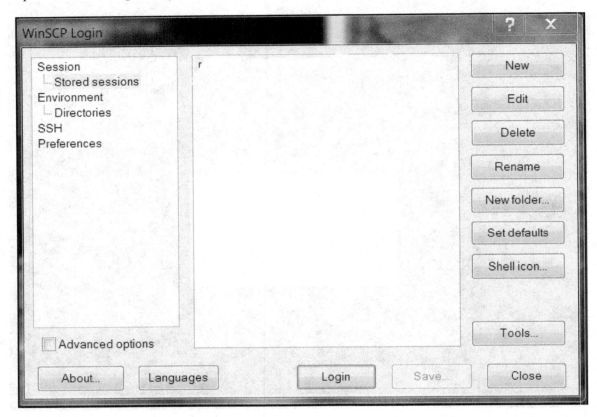

Click on **New** and you will get the following:

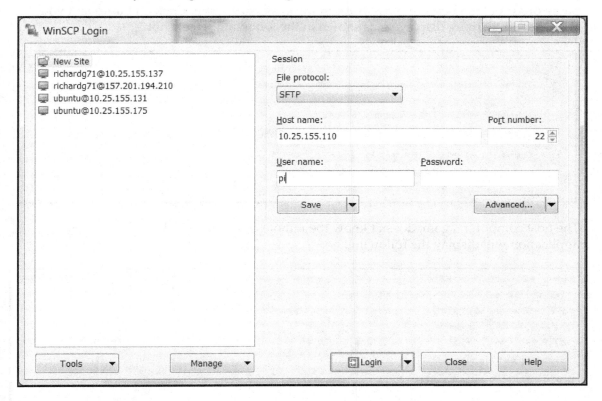

Here, you fill in the IP address in the **host name** tab, `pi` in the **user name** tab, and the password (not the vncserver password) in the **password** space. Click on **Login** and you should see a warning displayed, as shown in the following screenshot:

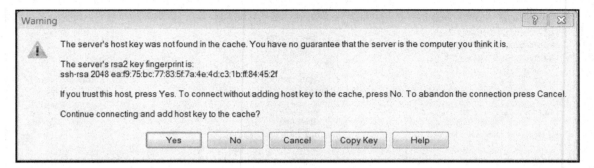

The host computer, again, doesn't know the remote computer. Click on **Yes** and the application will display the following:

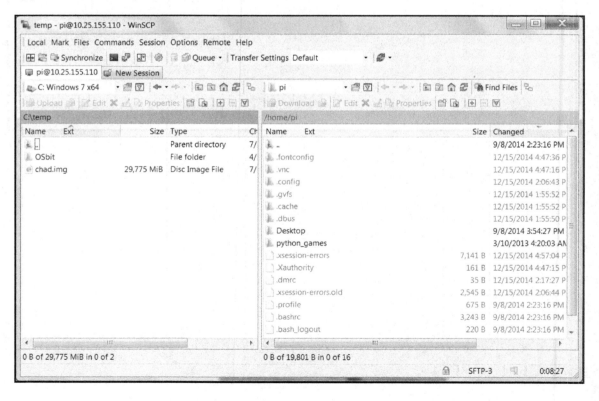

Now, you can drag and drop files from one system to the other. You can also do similar things with Linux by using the command line. To transfer a file to the remote Raspberry Pi, you can use the `scp file user@host.domain:path` command, where `file` is the filename, and `user@host.domain:path` is the location you want to copy it to. For example, if you wanted to copy `example.py` from your Linux system to the Raspberry Pi, you would type `scp example.py pi@10.25.155.176:/home/pi/`. The system will ask you for the remote password, which is the login for the Raspberry Pi. Enter the password and the file will be transferred.

Now that you know how to use `ssh`, `tightvncserver` and `scp`, you can access your Raspberry Pi remotely without having a display, keyboard, or mouse connected to it.

You only need to connect the power and the LAN, either with a cable or through wireless LAN. If you need to issue simple commands, connect through SSH. If you need a more complete set of graphical functionality, you can access this through `vncserver`. Finally, if you want to transfer files back and forth, you can use WinSCP from a Windows computer, or `scp` from a Linux computer. Now you have the toolkit to build your first functionality. You can also use scp on a Mac. Here is a link for more information: `https://research.csc.fi/csc-guide-copying-files-from-linux-and-mac-osx-machines-with-scp`.

One of the challenges of accessing the system remotely is that you need to know the IP address of your board. If you have the board connected to a keyboard and display, you can always just run the `ifconfig` command to get this information. However, you're going to use the board in applications in which you don't have this information. There is a way to discover this by using an IP scanner application. There are several available for free; on Windows, I use an application called Advanced IP Scanner, available at .

When you start the program, it looks like the following screenshot:

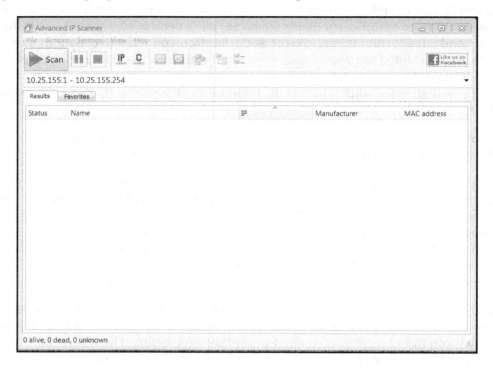

Clicking on the **Scan** selector scans for all the devices connected to the network. You can also do this in Linux; one application for IP scanning in Linux is called**Nmap**. To install Nmap, type `sudo apt-get install nmap`. To run Nmap, type `sudo nmap -sp 10.25.155.1/154` and the scanner will scan the addresses from `10.25.155.1` to `10.25.155.154`.

> For more information on Nmap, see `http://www.linux.com/learn/tuto rials/29879-beginners-guide-to-nmap`.

These scanners let you know which addresses are being used, and this should allow you to see your Raspberry Pi address without typing `ipconfig`. Your system has lots of capabilities. Feel free to play around with the system—try to get an understanding of what is already there and what you'll need to add from a software perspective.

Setting up the Raspberry Pi Zero

While the Raspberry Pi Zero is a powerful computer, you'll need some additional hardware to access this capability. Here are the items you'll need to set up the Raspberry Pi Zero:

- A Raspberry Pi Zero
- A micro USB cable and power supply to provide power to the board
- A display with an HDMI video input
- A keyboard, a mouse, and a powered USB hub
- A micro SD card – with at least 4 GB capacity
- A micro SD card writer
- Another computer that is connected to the Internet
- A WLAN USB dongle
- A 40×2 pin connector strip

Before you get started, let's get familiar with the Raspberry Pi Zero. Here is an image of the hardware:

Note that the GPIO pin male headers are not pre-soldered to the board; you'll want to do that. You can buy these at most online electronics retailers. You should also become familiar with the various connections on the board. Here, you can see the Raspberry Pi Zero with the connector soldered and the connections labeled for your information:

Powering the board

One of the first issues you'll want to consider is how to power the board. To do this, you need to connect through the USB power connection. The same two choices are available to power the Raspberry Pi Zero as the Raspberry Pi 3. However, you'll need to power the USB hub as well, so make sure you take that into account in your power choices.

Hooking up a keyboard, mouse, and display

The next step is to connect a keyboard, mouse, and display to the Raspberry Pi Zero. To connect any device to the Raspberry Pi Zero, you'll need some sort of adapter or hub. You can buy a simple hub, which goes from the micro USB connector on the Raspberry Pi Zero to the more common standard connector. You can find these at most online electronics retailers, and it looks something like the following:

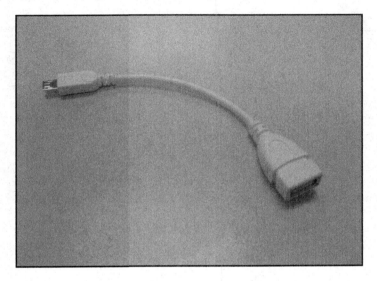

However, there will be projects when you will want to connect more than one device to the Raspberry Pi Zero. For these cases, you may want to consider purchasing a powered USB hub. Before deciding on the hub to connect to your board, you need to understand the difference between a powered USB hub and one that gets its power from the USB port itself.

Almost all USB hubs are unpowered. In other words, you don't plug in the USB hub separately. The reason for this is that almost all of these hubs are hooked up to computers with very large power supplies, and powering USB devices from the computer is not a problem. This is not the case for your board. The USB port on your board has very limited power capabilities, so if you are going to hook up devices that require significant power—a WAN adapter or a webcam, for instance—you're going to need a powered USB hub, one that provides power to the devices through a separate power source. Here is an image of such a device, available at http://www.amazon.com and other online retailers:

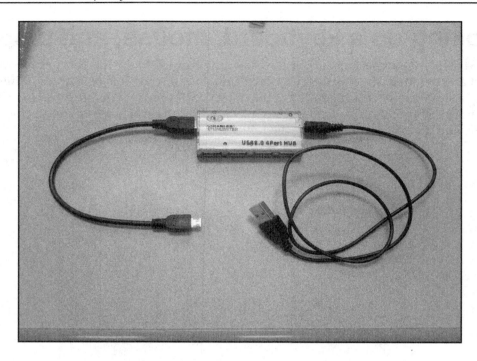

Note that there are two connections on this hub. The one to the far right is a power connection, which will be plugged into a battery or a USB power adapter with a USB port. The connection to the left is the USB connection, which will be plugged into the Raspberry Pi. To connect the powered USB board to the Raspberry Pi Zero, you need a cable that connects to a micro USB connector. Now, you'll have more connections to add a mouse and keyboard, webcams, and a USB WLAN device.

Now, you'll also need a display. There is a mini HDMI connector on the Raspberry Pi Zero. In order to connect it to an HDMI monitor, you'll need a mini HDMI to standard HDMI adapter or cable. You can also buy a cable that has a mini HDMI connector on one end and a regular HDMI connector on the other. Here is an image of the adapter:

To use this adapter, simply connect it to your Raspberry Pi Zero, then connect the cable with the regular HDMI connections to the adapter and your TV or monitor that has an HDMI input connector. As with the Raspberry Pi 3, you can also buy a cable that goes from mini HDMI to DVI.

So, connect your HDMI cable to your monitor and the Raspberry Pi Zero. Connect your USB hub to the Raspberry Pi Zero and connect your keyboard and mouse to the USB hub. Make sure that you connect all your devices before you power on the unit. Most operating systems support the hot-swap of devices, which means you are able to connect a device after the system has been powered on, but this is a bit shaky. You should always cycle power when you connect new hardware. Here is a picture of everything connected:

The USB connectors are connected to USB power adapters. Even though your hardware configuration is complete, you'll still need to complete the next section to power on the device. So, let's figure out how to install an operating system.

Installing the operating system

You'll create a micro SD card with the appropriate operating system, following the same instructions as for the Raspberry Pi 3. Make sure that your Raspberry Pi Zero is unplugged and install the SD card into the slot. Then power on the device. After the device boots, you should get the following screen:

You are up and running!

 Note that if you use a powered USB hub, it might provide enough power to your Raspberry Pi. However, in some circumstances, it might not be able to provide all the power you need. I strongly suggest you use different power sources—one for your Raspberry Pi Zero and one for your hub.

You should be ready to bring up a Terminal window and start typing commands.

Adding Internet access

Unlike the Raspberry Pi 3, the Raspberry Pi Zero does not have a LAN connection. To connect the Raspberry Pi Zero to the Internet, you have two choices. You can establish a wireless LAN connection, or you can connect by using a USB to LAN adapter if you want to connect to an actual LAN port. Let's look at both of these possibilities.

If you are going to connect wirelessly, make sure that you have a wireless access point available. You'll also need a wireless device. The official Raspberry Pi Foundation markets a device itself, but other brands also work.
See `http://elinux.org/RPi_USB_Wi-Fi_Adapters` to identify which wireless devices have been verified to work with the Raspberry Pi Zero. Here is one that is available at many online electronics outlets:

You'll also need to connect a powered USB hub for this process so that you can access both the keyboard and mouse, as well as the USB wireless LAN device. Now, connect the device to the powered hub.

Boot the system and then edit the `wpa_supplicant.conf` file by typing `sudo nano /etc/wpa_supplicant/wpa_supplicant.conf`. You need to change it to look like the following:

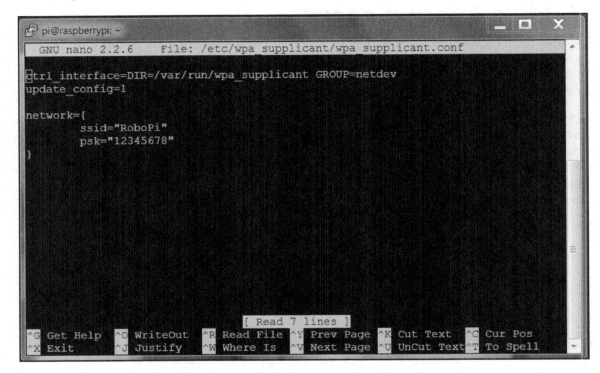

The `wpa-ssid` and `wpa-psk` values here must, of course, match what your wireless access point requires. Reboot and your device should be connected to your wireless network. You'll know if it is connected by looking in the upper right-hand corner of the screen, where you should see the following:

You can now download any additional functionality you want to install from the Internet.

If you want to connect to an actual LAN cabled connection, you need a device that goes from USB to LAN. This site, `http://elinux.org/RPi_USB_Ethernet_adapters`, lists a number of different possibilities. The following is an image of one such device:

Connecting the Raspberry Pi Zero in this way is actually amazingly easy. Simply plug the USB to LAN adapter into the powered USB hub, connect an active LAN cable, and you should have Internet access. You can then follow the same instructions as for the Raspberry Pi 3 to access your Raspberry Pi from your host PC.

Now that you know how to use `ssh`, `tightvncserver`, and `scp`, you can access your Raspberry Pi remotely without having a display, keyboard, or mouse connected to it! If you are connecting via a WLAN connection, your system will now look like the following:

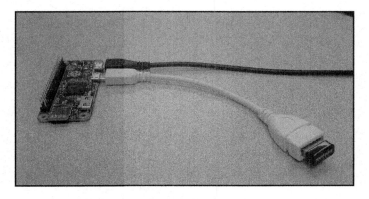

Now you can access your Raspberry Pi Zero remotely. As with the Raspberry Pi 3, you can use either the `ifconfig` command or Advanced IP Scanner to get the IP address of your Raspberry Pi Zero.

Summary

Congratulations! You've completed the first stage of your journey. You have your Raspberry Pi, either a 3 or a Zero, up and working. You have installed a Raspbian operating system, learned how to connect all the appropriate peripherals, and even mastered how to access the system remotely so that the only connections you need are a power supply cable and a LAN cable.

Now you are ready to start commanding your Raspberry Pi to do something. In the next chapter, you will be introduced to resources ranging including open source software and inexpensive hardware, and start to build your robotics projects. For the first project, you'll be building your very own R2D2.

2
Building Your Own Futuristic Robot

Now that you are up and running, let's start with a simple but impressive project in which you'll take a toy robot and give it much more functionality. You'll start with an R2D2 toy robot and modify it to add a webcam, voice recognition, and motors so that it can get around.

In this chapter, we'll cover the following topics:

- Using the Raspberry Pi to control two DC motors
- Hooking up the hardware to make and input sound
- Using eSpeak to allow our projects to respond with a robot voice
- Using PocketSphinx to accept your voice commands
- Using Python and the other tools to interpret commands and initiate actions
- Hooking up a USB webcam so that you can add vision to your project
- Downloading and configuring OpenCV so that your project can use this amazing open source software to detect objects, faces, colors, and motion

Creating your own R2D2 will require a bit of mechanical work; you'll need a drill and perhaps a Dremel tool, but most of the mechanical work will be removing the parts you don't need so you can add some exciting new capabilities.

Modifying the R2D2

There are several R2D2 toys that can provide the basis for this project. They are available from online retailers. This project will use one that is inexpensive but also provides such interesting features as a top that turns and a wonderful place to put a webcam. It is the Imperial Toy R2D2 bubble machine. Here is a picture of the unit:

The unit can be purchased at websites such as Amazon, Toys R Us, and a number of other e-retailers. It is normally used as a bubble machine that uses a canister of soap to produce bubbles, but you'll take all of that capability out to make your R2D2 much more like the original robot.

Adding wheels and motors

In order to make your R2D2 a reality, the first thing you'll want to do is add wheels to the robot. In order to do this, you'll need to take the robot apart, separating the two main plastic pieces that make up the lower body of the robot. Once you have done this, both the right and left arms can be removed from the body. You'll need to add two wheels that are controlled by DC motors to these arms.

Perhaps the best way to do this is to purchase a simple, two-wheeled car that is available at many online electronics stores, such as Amazon, Ebay, or Bandgood. Here is a picture of the parts that come with the car:

You'll be using these pieces to add mobility to your robot. The two yellow pieces are DC motors. So, let's start with those. To add these to the two arms on either side of the robot, you'll need to separate the two halves of the arm, and then remove material from one of the halves, like this:

You can use a Dremel tool to do this, or any kind of device that can cut plastic. This will leave a place for your wheel. Now you'll want to cut the plastic kit of your car up to provide a platform to connect to your R2D2 arm.

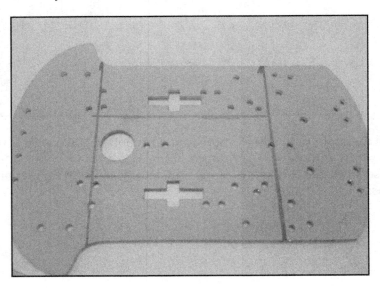

You'll cut your plastic car up using this as a pattern. You'll want to end up with the two pieces that have the + sign cutouts, and this is where you'll mount your wheels and also the piece you'll attach to the R2D2 arm. The following image will help you understand this better:

On the cut out side that has not been removed, mark and drill two holes to fix the clear plastic to the bottom of the arm. Fix the wheel to the plastic, then the plastic to the bottom of the arm, as shown in the picture. You'll connect two wires, one to each of the polarities on the motor, and then run the wires up to the top of the arm and out the small holes. These wires will eventually go into the body of the robot through small holes that you will drill where the arms connect to the body, like this:

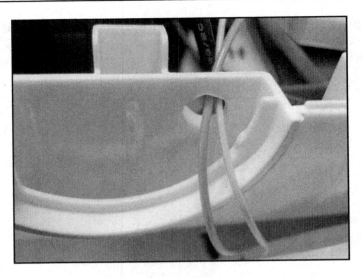

Repeat this process for the other arm. For the third, center arm, you'll want to connect the small, spinning white wheel to the bottom of the arm. Here is a picture:

Now that you have motors and wheels connected to the bottom of arms, you'll need to connect these to the Raspberry Pi. There are several different ways to connect and drive these two DC motors, but perhaps the easiest is to add a shield that can directly drive a DC motor.

This motor shield is an additional piece of hardware that installs on the top of the Raspberry Pi and can source the voltage and current to power both motors.

 The RaspiRobot Board V3 is available online and can provide these signals. The specifics on the board can be found at http://www.monkmakes.com/rrb3/.

Here is a picture of the board:

The board will provide the drive signals for the motors on each of the wheels. The following are the steps to connect Raspberry Pi to the board:

1. First, connect the battery power connector to the power connector on the side of the board.
2. Next, connect the two wires from one of the motors to the L motor connectors on the board.
3. Connect the other two wires from the other motor to the R motor connectors on the board.

Once completed your connections should look like this:

The red and black wires go to the battery, the green and yellow to the left motor, and the blue and white to the right motor. Now you will be able to control both the speed and the direction of the motors through the motor control board.

Connecting to the top of the R2D2

This particular version of R2D2 also comes with a top part that moves with the aid of a DC motor that is already installed. You'll now build some circuitry that can move this motor forward and backward. To do this, you'll need to connect an H-bridge circuit to the Raspberry Pi.

An H-bridge is a fairly simple device. It basically consists of a set of switches and adds the additional functionality of allowing the direction of the current to be reversed so that the motor can either be run in the forward or the reverse direction.

You'll first need to get an H-bridge. One of the most common options is the L293 dual H-bridge chip. This chip will allow you to control the direction of the DC motor connected to the head of the R2D2; you'll also be able to control the light on the R2D2. Here is a picture:

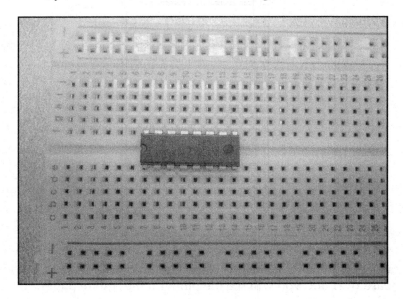

These are available at most electronics stores and online. Once you have your H-bridge, here is the basic circuit to control a motor and LED:

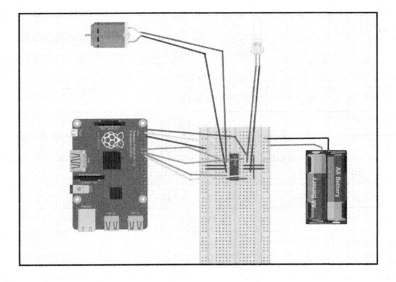

Also, before you start connecting wires, here is an image of the GPIO pins on the Raspberry Pi 3:

```
Pin 1 3.3V    □ ○   Pin 2 5V
Pin 3 GPIO2   ○ ○   Pin 4 5V
Pin 5 GPIO3   ○ ○   Pin 6 GND
Pin 7 GPIO4   ○ ○   Pin 8 GPIO14
Pin 9 GND     ○ ○   Pin 10 GPIO15
Pin 11 GPIO17 ○ ○   Pin 12 GPIO18
Pin 13 GPIO27 ○ ○   Pin 14 GND
Pin 15 GPIO22 ○ ○   Pin 16 GPIO23
Pin 17 3.3V   ○ ○   Pin 18 GPIO24
Pin 19 GPIO10 ○ ○   Pin 20 GND
Pin 21 GPIO9  ○ ○   Pin 22 GPIO25
Pin 23 GPIO11 ○ ○   Pin 24 GPIO8
Pin 25 GND    ○ ○   Pin 26 GPIO7
Pin 27 ID_SD  ○ ○   Pin 28 ID_SC
Pin 29 GPIO5  ○ ○   Pin 30 GND
Pin 31 GPIO6  ○ ○   Pin 32 GPIO12
Pin 33 GPIO13 ○ ○   Pin 34 GND
Pin 35 GPIO19 ○ ○   Pin 36 GPIO16
Pin 37 GPIO26 ○ ○   Pin 38 GPIO20
Pin 39 GND    ○ ○   Pin 40 GPIO21
```

Pin 1 on the Raspberry Pi GPIO is the one closest to the power on LED, but if you're not sure, flip the board over and you will see the pin with the square pattern. Pin 1 is also on the opposite end of the board from the USB connectors. Specifically, you'll want to connect these pins on the Raspberry Pi GPIO to the pins on the H-bridge, as shown in the following table:

Raspberry Pi GPIO pin	H-Bridge pin
Pin 4 (5V)	Pin 1 (enable pin)
Pin 13 (GPIO 27)	Pin 2 (forward)
Pin 15 (GPIO 22)	Pin 7 (backward)
Pin 4 (5V)	Pin 11 (enable 2)
Pin 38 (GPIO 6)	Pin 10 (forward)
Pin 40 (GPIO 13)	Pin 15 (backward)
Pin 6 (GND)	Pin 4, 5, 12, 13 (GND)
Pin 2 (5V)	Pin 16 (VCC)
Positive terminal from battery	Pin 8 (Vc)
Negative terminal from the battery	GND (connect to the same GND as previous GND pins)

Pin 3 and pin 5 on the H-bridge will go to the DC motor connector wires that control the DC motor. Here is a picture of the top of the R2D2, and the connections to this motor:

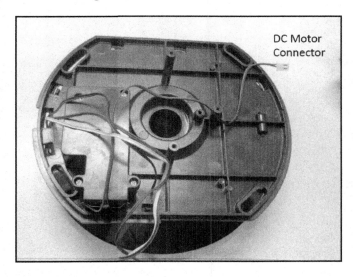

Once you have these connections, you can turn the top of R2D2. You can also trace the two wires that come from the LED and connect them to pins 12 and 14 on the H-bridge. Once they are connected, you'll need to add some code.

Controlling R2D2 using the Raspberry Pi in Python

The hardware is ready; now you can access all this functionality from the Raspberry Pi. First, install the library associated with the control board, found at `http://www.monkmakes.com/rrb3/`. Perform the following steps:

1. Type `cd ~`.
2. Run the command `git clone https://github.com/simonmonk/raspirobotboard3.git`—this will retrieve the library.
3. Then type `cd raspirobotboard3/python` to go to the `raspirobotboard3/python` directory.
4. Type `sudo python setup.py install`—this will install the files.
5. Now you'll create some Python code that will allow you to access both the DC

motor to turn the top and/or light the LED. Here is that code:

```
#!/usr/bin/python
import time
import RPi.GPIO as io
from rrb3 import *

io.setmode(io.BCM)

forward_pin = 27
backward_pin = 22
led1 = 24
led2 = 23

def forward():
    io.output(forward_pin, True)
    io.output(backward_pin, False)

def backward():
    io.output(forward_pin, False)
    io.output(backward_pin, True)

def stop():
    io.output(forward_pin, False)
    io.output(backward_pin, False)

rr = RRB3(9, 6)
io.setup(forward_pin, io.OUT)
io.setup(backward_pin, io.OUT)
io.setup(led1, io.OUT)
io.setup(led2, io.OUT)
stop()
io.output(led1, False)
io.output(led2, True)
time.sleep(1)
io.output(led1, False)
io.output(led2, False)
forward()
time.sleep(1)
backward()
time.sleep(1)
stop()
time.sleep(1)
rr.set_motors(1, 0, 1, 0)
time.sleep(1)
rr.set_motors(0, 0, 0, 0)
time.sleep(1)
rr.sw1_closed()
```

The first few lines of the code import the time, RPi.GPIO, and rrb3 libraries. The time library will allow you to delay your program, the RPi.GPIO library allows you to access the GPIO library, and the rrb3 library allows you access to the RaspiRobotBoard3.

The next lines of code set up the access to the pins you'll access to control the motor on the top part of the R2D2, as well as controlling the LED. The functions encapsulate the capability of turning the top forward or backward. The first few lines after the function initializes the setup of the RaspiRobotBoard3 and sets up the proper direction for the GPIO pins you're going to use.

The rest of the code exercises the functionality. The io.output led1 and led2 statements turns the LED on, then off. The forward() and reverse() function calls move the top of the R2D2 forward and backward. The rr.set_motors functions makes the wheels go forward.

When you have created the code, save it under the filename R2D2.py. Now you can run the program by typing python ./R2D2.py.

Since #!/usr/bin/python is on the first line of the program, if you make this program executable by typing chmod +x ./r2d2Arg.py, then you can run the program by simply typing ./r2d2Arg.py c.

The white LED on the top should turn on and then off, the top should turn one way and then back, and the wheels should move in the forward direction. This confirms that you have connected everything correctly. To make this a bit more interesting, you can add more dynamic control of the motors by adding some control code. Here is the Python code:

```python
#!/usr/bin/python

import time
import RPi.GPIO as io
from rrb3 import *
import termios
import sys
import tty

io.setmode(io.BCM)

forward_pin = 27
backward_pin = 22
led1 = 24
led2 = 23

def forward():
```

```
    io.output(forward_pin, True)
    io.output(backward_pin, False)

def backward():
    io.output(forward_pin, False)
    io.output(backward_pin, True)

def stop():
    io.output(forward_pin, False)
    io.output(backward_pin, False)
def getch():
    fd = sys.stdin.fileno()
    old_settings = termios.tcgetattr(fd)
    tty.setraw(sys.stdin.fileno())
    ch = sys.stdin.read(1)
    termios.tcsetattr(fd, termios.TCSADRAIN, old_settings)
    print '\n char is '' + ch + ''\n'
    return ch

rr = RRB3(9, 6)
io.setup(forward_pin, io.OUT)
io.setup(backward_pin, io.OUT)
io.setup(led1, io.OUT)
io.setup(led2, io.OUT)
#rr.set_oc1(1)

stop()
var = 'n'
print "starting up"
while var != 'q':
    var = getch()
    if var == 'c':
        io.output(led1, False)
        io.output(led2, True)
    if var == 'v':
        io.output(led1, False)
        io.output(led2, False)
    if var == 'f':
        rr.set_motors(1, 0, 1, 0)
    if var == 'b':
        rr.set_motors(1, 1, 1, 1)
    if var == 's':
        rr.set_motors(0, 0, 0, 0)
    if var == ',':
        rr.set_motors(1, 1, 1, 0)
    if var == '.':
        rr.set_motors(1, 0, 1, 1)
    if var == 'r':
```

```
        forward()
        time.sleep(1)
        stop()
    if var == 'l':
        backward()
        time.sleep(1)
        stop()
rr.sw1_closed()
```

Before you start, you may want to copy your `R2D2.py` Python code in a new file; you can call it `R2D2Control.py`. In this code, you'll have some additional import statements, `termios`, `sys`, and `tty`; these will allow you to sense key presses from the keyboard without hitting the *Enter* key, which will make the real-time interface seem more real-time. The `getch()` function senses the actual key press.

The second part of the code is a `while` loop that takes the input and translates it into commands for your R2D2, allowing the LED to turn off and on, moving the top, and moving R2D2 forward and backward and turning right and left. This program is quite simple; you'll almost certainly want to add more commands that provide more ways to control the speed and direction.

You may also want to call the R2D2 functions from another program, as you will when connecting to the speech recognition software. In this case, instead of processing key presses, you'll want to call the program with command-line arguments. Here is the Python code for that:

```python
#!/usr/bin/python
import time
import RPi.GPIO as io
from rrb3 import *
import sys

io.setmode(io.BCM)

forward_pin = 27
backward_pin = 22
led1 = 24
led2 = 23

def forward():
    io.output(forward_pin, True)
    io.output(backward_pin, False)

def backward():
    io.output(forward_pin, False)
    io.output(backward_pin, True)
```

```
def stop():
    io.output(forward_pin, False)
    io.output(backward_pin, False)

rr = RRB3(9, 6)
io.setup(forward_pin, io.OUT)
io.setup(backward_pin, io.OUT)
io.setup(led1, io.OUT)
io.setup(led2, io.OUT)
stop()
if (sys.argv[1]) == "c":
    io.output(led1, False)
    io.output(led2, True)
if (sys.argv[1]) == "v":
    io.output(led1, False)
    io.output(led2, False)
if (sys.argv[1]) == "f":
    rr.set_motors(1, 0, 1, 0)
    time.sleep(1)
    rr.set_motors(0, 0, 0, 0)
if (sys.argv[1]) == "b":
    rr.set_motors(1, 1, 1, 0)
    time.sleep(1)
    rr.set_motors(0, 0, 0, 0)
if (sys.argv[1]) == "s":
    rr.set_motors(0, 0, 0, 0)
if (sys.argv[1]) == "k":
    forward()
    time.sleep(1)
    stop()
if (sys.argv[1]) == "l":
    backward()
    time.sleep(1)
    stop()
rr.sw1_closed()
```

Again, you may want to start with the basic r2d2.py program and then add the additional capability. You'll add import sys so that you have access to the system arguments, or the arguments you type at the command line when you type the name of the program. You'll also need the set of if statements at the end of the program so that your robot will respond based on the command you type. Save this program under the name r2d2Arg.py

For example, if you type python ./r2d2Arg.py c the LED light should turn on. If you type python ./r2d2Arg.py c, the light will turn off. If you type python ./r2d2Arg.py f, your robot will go forward for one second. You can see how the rest of the commands work.

Adding voice recognition

Now that your robot is mobile, it is time to allow your robot to speak and respond to voice commands as well. This will make your R2D2 more interactive. To do this, you'll need to add some hardware. This project requires a USB microphone and a speaker adapter. The Raspberry Pi has an audio output, but does not have an audio input, so you'll need the following three pieces of hardware:

- A USB device that supports microphone in and speaker out:

- A microphone that can plug into the USB device:

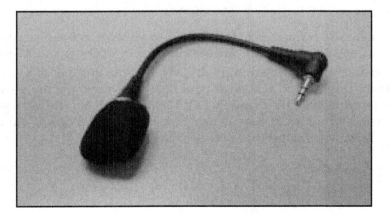

- A powered speaker that can plug into the USB device. In particular, you'll want one that has an internal battery that can connect to a USB port for charging, like this:

Fortunately, these devices are very inexpensive and widely available.

 Make sure the speaker is powered because your board will generally not be able to drive a passive speaker with enough power for your applications.

Now, on to allowing the Raspberry Pi access to these devices. You can execute all of the following instructions in one of the following ways:

- If you are still connected to the display, keyboard, and mouse, log into the system, and use the graphical user interface by opening an LXTerminal window.
- If you are only connected through LAN, you can do all of this using an SSH terminal window; so as soon as your board flashes that it has power, open up an SSH terminal window using PuTTY, or some similar Terminal emulator, if you are using Windows. If you are using a Linux or Mac system, you can simply open up a Terminal and use the SSH capability.

Plug the devices into a USB port. Once the Terminal window opens, type in `cat /proc/asound/cards`. You should see the following response:

```
pi@raspberrypi: ~
pi@raspberrypi:~$ cat /proc/asound/cards
 0 [ALSA          ]: bcm2835 - bcm2835 ALSA
                     bcm2835 ALSA
 1 [Device        ]: USB-Audio - C-Media USB Audio Device
                     C-Media USB Audio Device at usb-3f980000.usb-1.2, full speed
```

There are two possible audio devices. The first is the internal Raspberry Pi audio connected to the audio port, and the second is your USB audio plugin. You could use the USB audio plugin to record sound and the Raspberry Pi audio out to play the sound; it is easier to just use the USB audio plugin to both create and record sound.

First, you will play some music to test if the USB sound device is working. You'll need to configure your system to look for your USB audio plugin, and use it as the default plugin to play and record sound. To enable your sound system on Raspberry Pi, you'll first need to install some files that help provide the sound library by typing this command:

```
sudo apt-get install libasound2-dev.
```

You'll use an application named **alsamixer** to control the volume of both the input and the output of your USB sound card. To do this, perform the following steps:

1. Type `alsamixer` in the Command Prompt. You should see a screen that will look like the following screenshot:

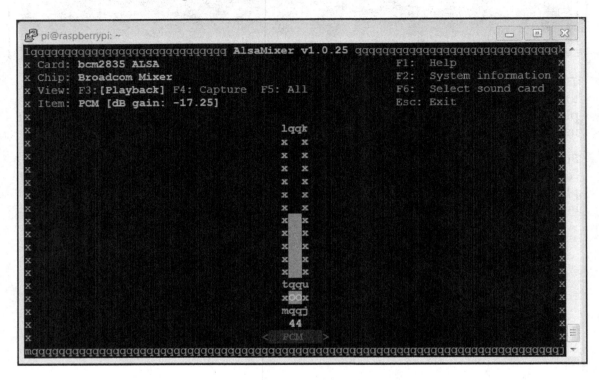

2. Press *F6* and select your USB sound device using the arrow keys. For example, refer to the following screenshot:

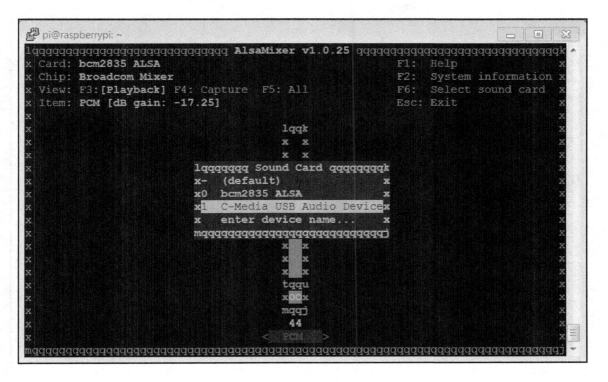

3. **C-Media USB Audio Device** area is my USB audio device. You should now see a screen that looks like the following screenshot:

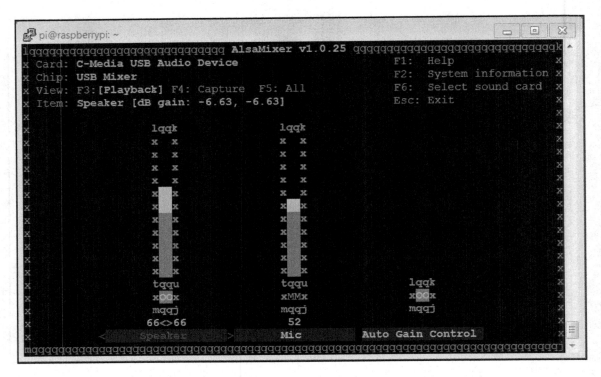

4. You can use the arrow keys to set the volume for both the speakers and the microphone. Use the *M* key to unmute the microphone. In the preceding screenshot, MM is mute and oo is unmute.

Let's make sure that our system knows about our USB sound device. In the Command Prompt, type `aplay -l`. You should now see the following screenshot:

```
pi@raspberrypi: ~
pi@raspberrypi:~$ aplay -l
**** List of PLAYBACK Hardware Devices ****
card 0: ALSA [bcm2835 ALSA], device 0: bcm2835 ALSA [bcm2835 ALSA]
  Subdevices: 8/8
  Subdevice #0: subdevice #0
  Subdevice #1: subdevice #1
  Subdevice #2: subdevice #2
  Subdevice #3: subdevice #3
  Subdevice #4: subdevice #4
  Subdevice #5: subdevice #5
  Subdevice #6: subdevice #6
  Subdevice #7: subdevice #7
card 0: ALSA [bcm2835 ALSA], device 1: bcm2835 ALSA [bcm2835 IEC958/HDMI]
  Subdevices: 1/1
  Subdevice #0: subdevice #0
card 1: Device [C-Media USB Audio Device], device 0: USB Audio [USB Audio]
  Subdevices: 1/1
  Subdevice #0: subdevice #0
pi@raspberrypi:~$ 
```

If this did not work, try `sudo aplay -l`. You are going to add a file to your home directory with the name `.asoundrc`. This will be read by your system and will be used to set your default configuration. To do this, perform the following steps:

1. Open the file named `.asoundrc` using your favorite editor. I prefer emacs, but nano and vi are also editors that are well documented.

2. Type in `pcm.!default sysdefault:Device`. `Device` is the variable that appears right after card 1, in the output of the `aplay -l` command.

3. Save the file.

This will tell the system to use your USB device as default. Reboot your system again.

Now you can play some music. To do this, you need a sound file and a device to play it. Copy a simple .wav file to your Raspberry Pi. If you are using a Linux machine as your host, you can also use scp from the command line to transfer the file. You can just download some music to Raspberry Pi using a web browser if you have a keyboard, mouse, and display connected, or you can use wget over SSH if you know the URL of the music you wish to download. You are going to use the application named aplay to play your sound. Type aplay Dance.wav to see if you can play music using the aplay music player. You will see the result (and hopefully hear it), as shown in the following screenshot:

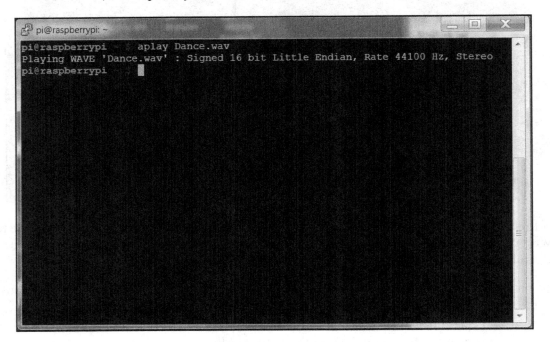

If you don't hear any music, check the volume you set with alsamixer and the power cable of your speaker. Also, aplay can be a bit finicky about the type of file it accepts, so you may have to try different .wav files until aplay accepts one. One more thing to try if the system doesn't seem to know about the program is to type sudo aplay Dance.wav.

Now you can play music or other sound files using your Raspberry Pi. You can change the volume of your speaker, and record your voice or other sounds on the system. You're now ready for the next step.

Using eSpeak to allow your robot to speak

Sound is an important tool in our robotic toolkit, but you will want to do more than just play music. Let's make our robot speak. You're going to start by enabling eSpeak, an open source application that provides us with a computer voice. eSpeak is an open source voice generation application. To get this free functionality, download the eSpeak library by typing `sudo apt-get install espeak` in the prompt. The download may take a while, but the prompt will reappear when it is complete. Now, let's see if our Raspberry Pi has a voice. Type the `espeak "hello"` command. The speaker should emit a computer-voiced hello. If it does not, check the speakers and the volume level.

Now that we have a computer voice, you may want to customize it. eSpeak offers a fairly complete set of customization features, including a large number of languages, voices, and other options. To access these, you can type in the options at the command prompt. For example, type in `espeak -v+f3 "hello"` and you should hear a female voice. You can add a Scottish accent by typing `espeak -ven-sc+f3 "hello"`.

There are a lot of choices with respect to the voices you might use with `espeak`. Feel free to play around and choose your favorite. Then, edit the default file to set it to that voice. However, don't expect that you'll get the kind of voices that you hear from computers in the movies; those are actors and not computers, although one day we will hopefully reach a stage where computers will sound a lot more like real people.

Using PocketSphinx to accept your voice commands

Now that your robot can speak, you'll want it to also obey voice commands. This section will show you how to add speech recognition to your robotic projects. This isn't nearly as simple as the speaking part, but thankfully, you have some significant help from the open source development community. You are going to download a set of capabilities named PocketSphinx, which will allow our project to listen to our commands.

The first step is downloading the PocketSphinx capabilities. Unfortunately, this is not quite as user friendly as the `espeak` process, so follow along carefully. There are two possible ways to do this. If you have a keyboard, mouse, and display connected, or want to connect through vncserver, you can do this graphically by performing the following steps:

1. Go to the Sphinx website hosted by Carnegie Mellon University (CMU) at `http://cmusphinx.sourceforge.net/` using a web browser window. This is an open source project that provides you with the speech recognition software. With our smaller, embedded system, we will be using the PocketSphinx version of this code.

2. You will need to download two software modules – sphinxbase and PocketSphinx. Select the **Download** option at the top of the page and then find an acceptable version of both of these packages. The one that is most stable at the time of writing is 0.8. Download the `.tar.gz` version of these and move them to the `/home/pi` directory of your Raspberry Pi.

Another way to accomplish this is to use `wget` directly from the Command Prompt of the Raspberry Pi. If you want to do it this way, perform the following steps:

1. To use `wget` on your Raspberry Pi, find the link to the file you wish to download. In this case, go to the Sphinx website hosted by CMU at `http://cmusphinx.sourceforge.net/`. This is an open source project that provides you with the speech recognition software. With your smaller, embedded system, you will be using the PocketSphinx version of this code.

2. You will need to download two software modules, namely sphinxbase and PocketSphinx. Select the **Download** option at the top of the page and then find the latest stable version of both these packages. Right-click on the `sphinxbase-0.8.tar.gz` file (if this is the latest stable version) and select **Copy Link Location**. Now open an SSH connection to the Raspberry Pi, and after logging in, type `wget` and paste the link you just copied. This will download the `.tar.gz` version of sphinxbase. Now follow the same procedure with the latest version of PocketSphinx.

Before you build these, you need two libraries. The first library is libasound2-dev. Type `sudo apt-get install libasound2-dev`. The second library is called Bison. This is a general purpose, open source parser that will be used by PocketSphinx. To get this package, type `sudo apt-get install bison`. You'll also need `sudo apt-get install python-dev`.

Once everything is installed and downloaded, you can build PocketSphinx. To unpack and build the sphinxbase module, type `sudo tar -xzvf sphinxbase-0.8.tar.gz`. This should unpack all the files from the archive into a directory named `sphinxbase-0.8`. Now move to the new directory created by unpacking the file.

To build the application, start by issuing the `sudo ./configure --enable-fixed` command. This command will check that everything is okay with the system, and then configure a build.

Now you are ready to actually build the `sphinxbase` code base. This is a two-step process, which is as follows:

1. Type `sudo make`, and the system will build all the executable files.
2. Type `sudo make install`, and this will install all the executables onto the system.

Now you need to make the second part of the system – the `pocketSphinx` code itself. Go to the home directory, and decompress and unarchive the code by typing `tar -xzvf pocketsphinx-0.8.tar.gz`. The files should now be unarchived, and you can now build the code. Installing these files is a three-step process, as follows:

1. Type `cd pocketsphinx-0.8` to go to the `pocketSphinx-0.8` directory, and then type `sudo ./configure` to see if you are ready to build the files.
2. Type `sudo make` and wait for a while for everything to build.
3. Type `sudo make install`.

Several possible additions to your library installations will be useful later if you are going to use your PocketSphinx capability with Python as a coding language. You can get Cython using `sudo apt-get install cython`. You can also choose to install `pkg-config`, a utility that can sometimes help deal with complex compiles. Install it using `sudo apt-get install pkg-config`.

Once the installation is complete, you'll need to let the system know where your files are. To do this, you will need to edit the /etc/ld.so.conf path as the root by typing sudo emacs /etc/ld.so.conf. You will add the last line to the file, so it should now look like the following screenshot:

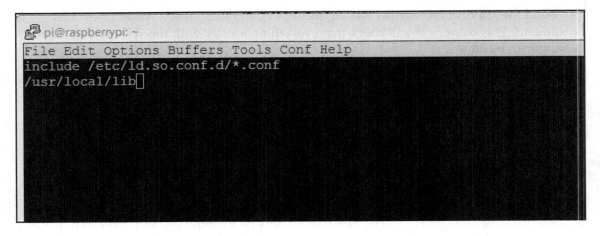

Now type sudo /sbin/ldconfig, and the system will now be aware of your PocketSphinx libraries. You may want to reboot at this point, just to make sure everything is installed and set up.

Now that everything is installed, you can try our speech recognition. Reboot the system, then type cd /home/pi/pocketsphinx-0.8/src/programs to go to a directory to try a demo program; then type ./pocketsphinx_continuous. This program takes input from the microphone and turns it into speech.

After running the command, you'll get a lot of irrelevant information, and then you will see the following screenshot:

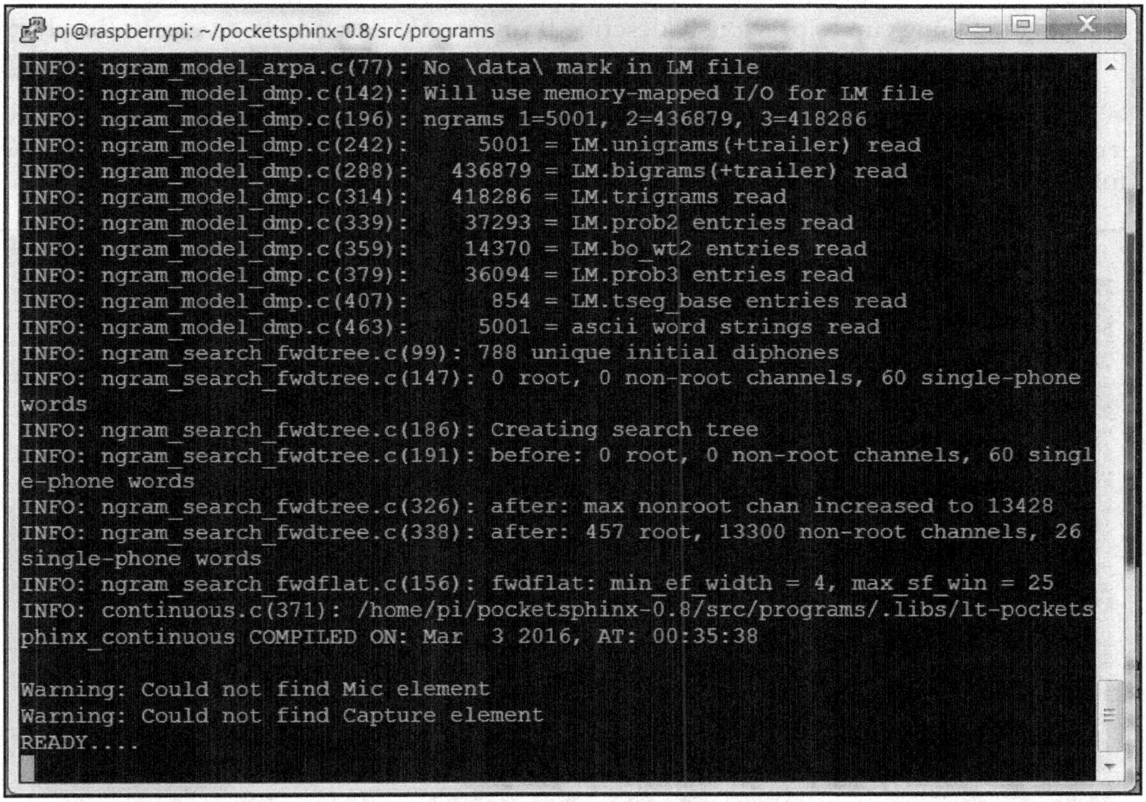

```
pi@raspberrypi: ~/pocketsphinx-0.8/src/programs
INFO: ngram_model_arpa.c(77): No \data\ mark in LM file
INFO: ngram_model_dmp.c(142): Will use memory-mapped I/O for LM file
INFO: ngram_model_dmp.c(196): ngrams 1=5001, 2=436879, 3=418286
INFO: ngram_model_dmp.c(242):     5001 = LM.unigrams(+trailer) read
INFO: ngram_model_dmp.c(288):   436879 = LM.bigrams(+trailer) read
INFO: ngram_model_dmp.c(314):   418286 = LM.trigrams read
INFO: ngram_model_dmp.c(339):    37293 = LM.prob2 entries read
INFO: ngram_model_dmp.c(359):    14370 = LM.bo_wt2 entries read
INFO: ngram_model_dmp.c(379):    36094 = LM.prob3 entries read
INFO: ngram_model_dmp.c(407):      854 = LM.tseg_base entries read
INFO: ngram_model_dmp.c(463):     5001 = ascii word strings read
INFO: ngram_search_fwdtree.c(99): 788 unique initial diphones
INFO: ngram_search_fwdtree.c(147): 0 root, 0 non-root channels, 60 single-phone
words
INFO: ngram_search_fwdtree.c(186): Creating search tree
INFO: ngram_search_fwdtree.c(191): before: 0 root, 0 non-root channels, 60 singl
e-phone words
INFO: ngram_search_fwdtree.c(326): after: max nonroot chan increased to 13428
INFO: ngram_search_fwdtree.c(338): after: 457 root, 13300 non-root channels, 26
single-phone words
INFO: ngram_search_fwdflat.c(156): fwdflat: min_ef_width = 4, max_sf_win = 25
INFO: continuous.c(371): /home/pi/pocketsphinx-0.8/src/programs/.libs/lt-pockets
phinx_continuous COMPILED ON: Mar  3 2016, AT: 00:35:38

Warning: Could not find Mic element
Warning: Could not find Capture element
READY....
```

The INFO and Warning statements come from the C or C++ code and are there for debugging purposes. Initially, they will warn you that they cannot find your Mic and Capture elements, but when the Raspberry Pi finds them, it will print out READY . . . . . If you have set things up as previously described, you should be ready to give your Raspberry Pi a command. Say *hello* into the microphone.

When it senses that you have stopped speaking, it will process your speech and give lots of irrelevant information again, but it should eventually show the commands, as shown in the following screenshot:

```
pi@raspberrypi: ~/pocketsphinx-0.8/src/programs
INFO: ngram_search_fwdtree.c(1549):     3060 words recognized (34/fr)
INFO: ngram_search_fwdtree.c(1551):   262701 senones evaluated (2887/fr)
INFO: ngram_search_fwdtree.c(1553):   410539 channels searched (4511/fr), 38015
1st, 101765 last
INFO: ngram_search_fwdtree.c(1557):     6228 words for which last channels evalu
ated (68/fr)
INFO: ngram_search_fwdtree.c(1560):    31727 candidate words for entering last p
hone (348/fr)
INFO: ngram_search_fwdtree.c(1562): fwdtree 0.96 CPU 1.055 xRT
INFO: ngram_search_fwdtree.c(1565): fwdtree 2.26 wall 2.487 xRT
INFO: ngram_search_fwdflat.c(302): Utterance vocabulary contains 154 words
INFO: ngram_search_fwdflat.c(937):     2216 words recognized (24/fr)
INFO: ngram_search_fwdflat.c(939):    94876 senones evaluated (1043/fr)
INFO: ngram_search_fwdflat.c(941):   184625 channels searched (2028/fr)
INFO: ngram_search_fwdflat.c(943):     9581 words searched (105/fr)
INFO: ngram_search_fwdflat.c(945):     7225 word transitions (79/fr)
INFO: ngram_search_fwdflat.c(948): fwdflat 0.39 CPU 0.429 xRT
INFO: ngram_search_fwdflat.c(951): fwdflat 0.39 wall 0.426 xRT
INFO: ngram_search.c(1266): lattice start node <s>.0 end node </s>.77
INFO: ngram_search.c(1294): Eliminated 0 nodes before end node
INFO: ngram_search.c(1399): Lattice has 265 nodes, 780 links
INFO: ps_lattice.c(1365): Normalizer P(O) = alpha(</s>:77:89) = -651639
INFO: ps_lattice.c(1403): Joint P(O,S) = -656946 P(S|O) = -5307
INFO: ngram_search.c(888): bestpath 0.01 CPU 0.011 xRT
INFO: ngram_search.c(891): bestpath 0.01 wall 0.015 xRT
000000003: hello
READY....
```

Notice the 000000003: hello command. It recognized your speech! You can try other words and phrases too. The system is very sensitive, so it may pick up background noise. You are also going to find that it is not very accurate. We'll deal with that in a moment. To stop the program, type ctrl-c.

There are two ways to make your voice recognition more accurate. One is to train the system to understand your voice more accurately. This is a bit complex, but if you want to know more, go to the PocketSphinx website of CMU.

The second way to improve accuracy is to limit the number of words that your system uses to determine what you are saying. The default has literally thousands of word possibilities, so if two words are close, PocketSphinx may choose the wrong word. To avoid this, you can make your own dictionary to restrict the words it has to choose from. To do this, go to `http://www.speech.cs.cmu.edu/tools/lmtool-new.html`. Once there, you can upload a `.txt` file with the desired words you want to be able to decode. For example, here is a file with many of the words you might want your R2D2 to recognize:

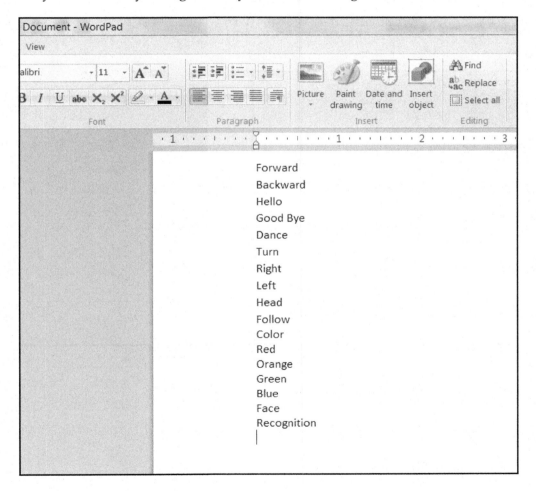

Now that you have the file, save it as a text file. Then upload the text file to the website and press the **Compile Data Base selection**. You should then see this screen:

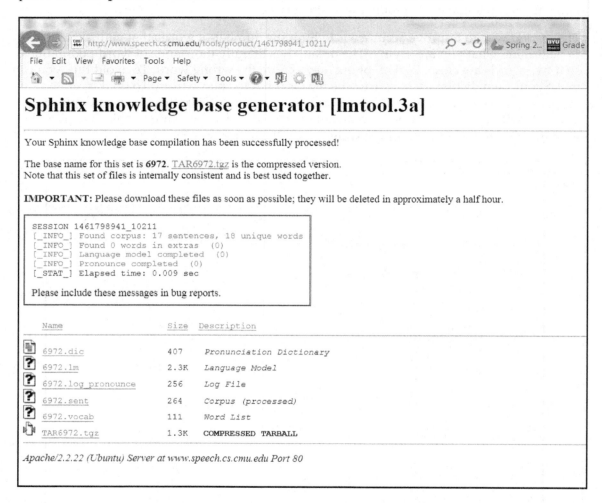

Now download the TAR file, in this case, `TAR6972.tgz`. Once you have this file on the Raspberry Pi you can untar it to a directory; in this case, you can call it `dictionary6972`. In that directory you should now see the following:

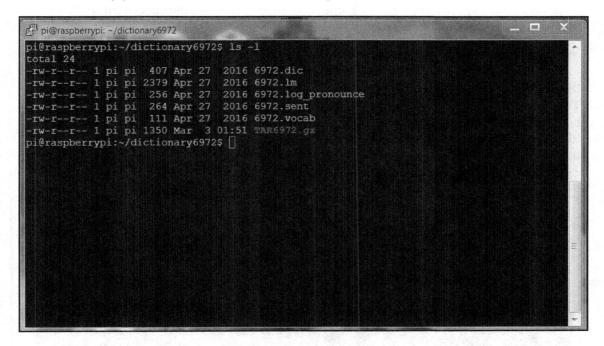

This will have all the files you'll need for your custom grammar. To run the PocketSphinx continuous program with this dictionary, type `./pocketsphinx_continuous -dict /home/pi/dictionary6972/6972.dic -lm /home/pi/dictionary6972/6972.lm` and the program will run with this dictionary.

Your system can now understand your specific voice commands! In the next section of this chapter, you'll learn how to use this input to have the project respond.

Interpreting commands and initiating actions

Now that the system can both hear and speak, you'll want to provide the capability to respond to your speech and execute some commands based on the speech input. Next, you're going to configure the system to respond to simple commands.

In order to respond, you're going to edit the `continuous.c` code in the `/home/pi/ pocketsphinx-0.8/src/programs` directory. You could create our own C file, but this file is already set up in the `makefile` system and is an excellent starting spot. You can save a copy of the current file in `continuous.c.old` so that you can always get back to the starting program, if required. Then, you will need to edit the `continuous.c` file. It is very long and a bit complicated, but you are specifically looking for the section in the code, which is shown in the following screenshot. Look for the `/* Exit if the first word spoken was GOODBYE */` comment line:

```
pi@raspberrypi: ~/pocketsphinx-0.8/src/programs
File Edit Options Buffers Tools C Help
        ps_end_utt(ps);
        hyp = ps_get_hyp(ps, NULL, &uttid);
        printf("%s: %s\n", uttid, hyp);
        fflush(stdout);

        /* Exit if the first word spoken was GOODBYE */
        if (hyp) {
            sscanf(hyp, "%s", word);
            if (strcmp(word, "goodbye") == 0)
                break;
        }

        /* Resume A/D recording for next utterance */
        if (ad_start_rec(ad) < 0)
            E_FATAL("Failed to start recording\n");
    }

    cont_ad_close(cont);
    ad_close(ad);
}
-UU-:----F1  continuous.c    82% L331    (C/1 Abbrev)----------------------------
```

In this section of the code, the word has already been decoded and is held in the `hyp` variable. You can add code here to make your system do things based on the value associated with the word which we have decoded. First, let's try adding the capability to respond to *hello* and *goodbye* to see if we can get the program to respond to these commands. You'll need to make changes to the code in the following manner:

```
if (hyp) {
    sscanf(hyp, "%s", word);
    if (strcmp(word, "GOOD") == 0)
        {
            system ("espeak "good bye"");
            break;
        }
    if (strcmp(word, "HELLO") == 0)
        {
            system ("aplay /home/pi/R2D2.wav");
        }

}
```

Now you need to rebuild your code. As the `make` system already knows how to build the `pocketsphinx_continuous` program, it will rebuild the application if you make a change to the `continuous.c` file at any point in time. Simply type `sudo make`, and the file will compile and create a new version of `pocketsphinx_continuous`. To run your new version, type `sudo ./pocketsphinx_continuous -dict /home/pi/dictionary6972/6972.dic -lm /home/pi/dictionary6972/6972.lm`. Make sure you type the `./` at the start. The first time you run this, it will fail. Then simply type `./pocketsphinx_continuous -dict /home/pi/dictionary6972/6972.dic -lm /home/pi/dictionary6972/6972.lm` and it will run. In this case, I downloaded a WAV file from the Internet with R2D2 sounds in it, and placed that in my home directory. If everything is set correctly, saying *hello* should result in a response of an R2D2 `hello` from your Raspberry Pi. Saying *good bye* should elicit a response of `good bye` and also shut down the program. Notice that the system command can be used to run any program that runs with a command line. Now you can use this program to start and run other programs based on the commands. In this case, you'll want to change this part of the code to call your Python code to issue commands to the robot, like this:

```
if (hyp) {
    sscanf(hyp, "%s", word);
    if (strcmp(word, "GOOD") == 0)
        {
            system ("espeak "good bye"");
            break;
        }
```

```
if (strcmp(word, "HELLO") == 0)
    {
        system ("aplay /home/pi/R2D2.wav");
    }
if (strcmp(word, "FORWARD") == 0)
    {
        system ("/home/pi/r2d2/r2d2Arg.py f");
    }
if (strcmp(word, "BACKWARD") == 0)
    {
        system ("/home/pi/r2d2/r2d2Arg.py b");
    }
}
```

This code connects just two of the commands that your robot could respond to from your previous r2d2Arg.py program; you can add the rest of the commands to continuous.c using this same technique. Now you can give your robot voice commands and it will obey them!

Adding video capability

No self-respecting R2D2 robot would be complete without the ability to see. Fortunately, your R2D2 has just the right spot for a webcam. Once you remove the bubble blowing port, you have the perfect spot for a round webcam.

Here is a picture of a round webcam, which is available on amazon.com and other online retailers:

Here is a picture of the webcam mounted in the slot:

You now need to connect the USB camera to the USB port of the Raspberry Pi. To access the USB webcam directly on the Raspberry Pi, you can use a Linux program called `guvcview`. Install this by powering up the Raspberry Pi, logging in, and entering the `sudo apt-get install guvcview` command.

To try your USB camera, connect it and reboot your Raspberry Pi. To check if the Raspberry Pi has found your USB camera, go to the /dev directory and type ls. You should see something similar to the following screenshot:

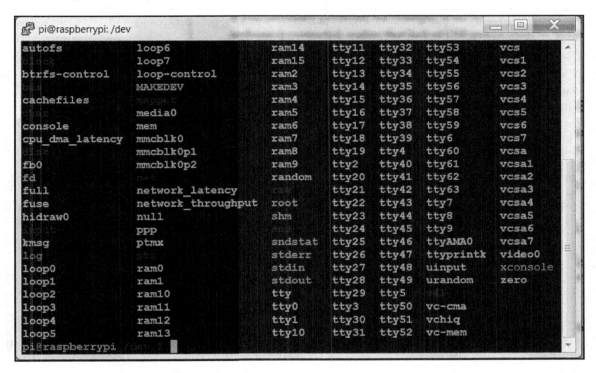

Look for video0, as this is the entry for your webcam. If you see it, the system knows your camera is there.

Now, let's use `guvcview` to see the output of the camera. Since it will need to output some graphics, you either need to use a monitor connected to the board, as well as a keyboard and mouse, or you can use vncserver as described in `Chapter 1`, *Getting Started with the Raspberry Pi*. Eventually, you will want to use the wireless access point capability described in the first chapter anyway, so the best course of action is to connect your host computer to the wireless access point, SSH into the Raspberry Pi, then start the vncserver on the Raspberry Pi by typing vncserver through SSH. Then, start up VNC Viewer as described in `Chapter 1`, *Getting Started with the Raspberry Pi*. With all these tools installed, you can now run `vncview`. When you are viewing the graphical screen of the Raspberry Pi Zero, type `guvcivew -r 2`, and you will be able to see the video from the webcam.

You can control your R2D2 remotely by running the `r2d2Control.py` program that you wrote earlier. The screen will look similar to the following screenshot:

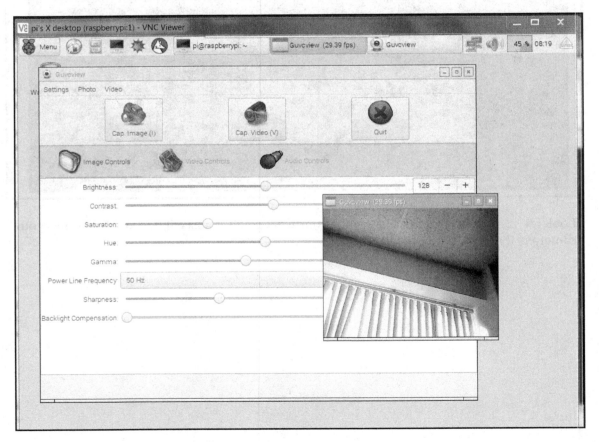

You will notice that as you adjust the resolution down, the update rate goes up; this is related to the size of the image.

The video window displays what the webcam sees, and the **GUVCViewer Controls** window controls the different characteristics of the camera. The default settings of the camera work fine. However, if you get a black screen for the camera, you may need to adjust the settings. Select the **GUVCViewer Controls** window and the **Video & Files** tab. You will see a window where you can adjust the settings for your camera.

The most important setting is **Resolution**. If you see a black screen, lower the resolution; this will often resolve the issue. This window will also tell you what resolutions are supported by your camera. Also, you can display the frame rate by checking the box to the right of the **Frame Rate** setting. Be aware, however, that if you are going through vncviewer, the refresh rate (how quickly the video window will update itself) will be much slower than if you're using a Raspberry Pi and a monitor directly.

Once you have the camera up and running, and the desired resolution set, you can go on to download and install OpenCV.

 You can connect more than one webcam to the system. Follow the same steps, but connect to the cameras through a USB hub. List the devices in the /dev directory. Use guvcview to see the different images. One challenge, however, is that connecting too many cameras can overwhelm the bandwidth of the USB port.

Downloading and installing OpenCV – a fully featured vision library

Now that you have your camera connected, you can begin to access some amazing capabilities that have been provided by the open source community. The most popular of these for computer vision is OpenCV. To do this, you'll need to install OpenCV. There are several possible ways of doing this; I'm going to suggest the ones that I follow to install it on my system. Some of these packages may have already been installed based on earlier activities, but I'll document all the steps here. Once you have booted the system and opened a Terminal window, type the following commands in the given order:

1. `sudo apt-get update`: If you haven't done this in a while, it is a good idea to do this now, before you start. You're going to download a number of new software packages, so it is good to make sure that everything is up to date.

2. `sudo apt-get install build-essential`: You should have done this in a previous chapter. If you skipped that part, you will have to do it now, as you need this package.

3. `sudo apt-get install libavformat-dev`: This library provides a way to code and decode audio and video streams.

4. `sudo apt-get install libcv2.4 libcvaux2.4 libhighgui2.4`: This command shows the basic OpenCV libraries. Note the number in the command. This will almost certainly change as new versions of OpenCV become available; however, 2.4 is a very stable release.

5. `sudo apt-get install python-opencv`: This is the Python development kit needed for OpenCV, as you are going to use Python.

6. `sudo apt-get install opencv-doc`: This command will show the documentation for OpenCV, just in case you need it.

7. `sudo apt-get install libcv-dev`: This command shows the header file and static libraries to compile OpenCV.

8. `sudo apt-get install libcvaux-dev`: This command shows more development tools for compiling OpenCV.

9. `sudo apt-get install libhighgui-dev`: This is another package that provides header files and static libraries to compile OpenCV.

10. `sudo apt-get install libgl1-mesa-swx11`: This installs a substitute of OpenGL that you'll need when you want to access your OpenCV capabilities remotely through vncserver.

Now type `cp -r /usr/share/doc/opencv-doc/examples /home/pi/`. This will copy all the examples to your home directory.

Now you are ready to try out the OpenCV library. I prefer to use Python while programming simple tasks, hence I'll show the Python examples. If you prefer the C examples, feel free to explore.

Now that you have these, you can try one of the Python examples. Switch to the directory with the Python examples by typing `cd /home/pi/examples/python`. In this directory, you will find a number of useful examples; you'll only look at the most basic, which is called `camera.py`. You can run this example; however, to do this, since your Raspberry Pi is deep inside your R2D2, you'll want to do this over a vncserver connection, as described in `Chapter 1`, *Getting Started with the Raspberry Pi*.

Once you have the vncserver connection, bring up the Terminal window and type `python camera.py`. You should see something similar to the following screenshot:

The camera window is quite large; you can change the resolution of the image to a lower one, which will make the update rate faster, and the storage requirement for the image smaller. To do this, edit the `camera.py` file and add two lines, like this:

```python
#!/usr/bin/python

import cv2.cv as cv
import time

cv.NamedWindow("camera", 1)

capture = cv.CaptureFromCAM(0)
cv.SetCaptureProperty(capture, 3, 360)
cv.SetCaptureProperty(capture, 4, 240)

while True:
    img = cv.QueryFrame(capture)
    cv.ShowImage("camera", img)
    if cv.WaitKey(10) == 27:
```

```
        break
cv.DestroyAllWindows()
```

Here is an explanation of the Python code:

- `import cv2.cv as cv`: This line imports the OpenCV library so you can access its functionality.
- `import time`: This line imports the time library so you can access the time functionality.
- `cv.NamedWindow("camera", 1)`: This line creates a window that you will use to display your image.
- `capture = cvCaptureFromCAM(0)`: This line creates a structure that knows how to capture images from the connected webcam.
- `cv.SetCaptureProperty(capture, 3, 360)`: This line sets the image width to 360 pixels.
- `cv.SetCaptureProperty(capture, 4, 240)`: This line sets the image height to 240 pixels.
- `while True::` Here, you are creating a loop that will capture and display the image over and over again until you press the *Esc* key.
- `img = cv.QueryFrame(capture)`: This line captures the image and stores it in the `img` data structure.
- `cv.ShowImage("camera", img)`: This line maps the `img` variable to the camera window that you created previously.
- `If cv.WaitKey(10) == 27::` This `if` statement checks if a key has been pressed, and if the pressed key is the *Esc* key, it executes the break. This stops the `while` loop, and the program reaches its end and stops. You need this statement in your code because it also signals OpenCV to display the image now.

Now run `camera.py`, and you should see the following screenshot:

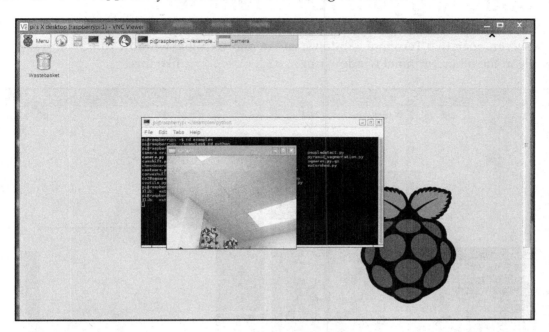

Now that you are up and running, you can use OpenCV to display and process images. You may want to play with the resolution to find the optimum settings for your application. Bigger images are great—they give you a more detailed view of the world—but they also take up significantly more processing power. You'll play with this more as you actually ask your system to do some real image processing. Be careful, if you are going to use vncserver, to understand your system performance, as this will significantly slow down the update rate. An image that is twice the size (width/height) will involve four times more processing.

Your project can now see! You will use this capability to remotely monitor and control your R2D2.

Controlling your R2D2 remotely

Now, via vncserver, you can access a video feed and control your robot. Simply access vncserver, open two Terminal windows, and in one Terminal window run `camera.py`, while in the other Terminal window run `r2d2Control.py`, like this:

In this instance, there is a third window so that you can use aplay to play R2D2 WAV files that you have downloaded from the Internet. Now you can remotely pilot your R2D2 from a host computer or tablet. If you'd like to do it via a tablet or phone, you'll want to download an SSH app; there are several available from the different app stores. You can use your Wi-Fi settings to connect to the R2D2 access point. Then run the SSH app to access your R2D2 and start vncserver. Then you'll need a vncviewer app; again, there are several available, to access your R2D2 and run a similar configuration from your tablet or phone.

OpenCV is an amazing, powerful library of functions. You can do all sorts of incredible things with just a few lines of code. A common feature that you may want to add to your projects is motion detection.

If you'd like to try, there are several good tutorials; try looking at the following links:

- http://derek.simkowiak.net/motion-tracking-with-python/
- http://stackoverflow.com/questions/3374828/how-do-i-track-motion-using-opencv-in-python
- https://www.youtube.com/watch?v=8QouvYMfmQo
- https://github.com/RobinDavid/Motion-detection-OpenCV

Having a webcam connected to your system provides all kinds of complex vision capabilities.

Summary

You've completed your first project, your own R2D2. You can now move it around, program it to respond to voice commands, or run it remotely from a computer, tablet, or phone. Following in this theme, your next robot will look and act like WALL-E.

3

Building a Wall-E Robot

Now that you've built an R2D2, and you know how to control DC motors and provide sight for your robot, now let's build a robot that you almost certainly have heard of. I am talking about Wall-E. Your robot will have some cool capabilities, including rolling around on two tracks, two arms that move, and a vision system that, thanks to the Microsoft Kinect, will give you not Now your arm with the hand is completeonly a video image but also a depth image.

In this chapter, you'll learn the following:

- Using the Raspberry Pi to control two DC motors for a track system
- Using an external servo controller to control servos to position simple arms and hands
- Creating a program in Linux to control servos and motors
- Adding the Microsoft Kinect 360 for not only vision but depth as well

Since you will be creating your own Wall-E without the benefit having the head start of an existing toy, it will be more difficult mechanically, but will provide a robot with lots of capabilities.

Creating the hardware platform

There are several inexpensive, basic tracked vehicles that can be the base for your robot. Here is a picture just such a unit:

The unit can be purchased at many different online electronics outlets, such as eBay, Amazon, Banggood, and other vendors. This example uses the Wali SUV SN1100 V2 available on eBay. It, of course, comes unassembled, so let's briefly look at how to build the unit. Here is a picture of all the parts:

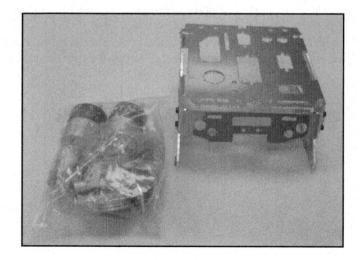

Here are the steps to assemble the unit:

1. The first step is to open up the plastic bag and look at all the parts. Here they are:

2. Now you'll need to put the wheels together. These fit inside the tracks. Two of them, the ones with the outer rim that is spoked, will be connected to the DC motors. But let's start with ones that don't have spikes on the outer rim. Here is a picture of one of the wheels assembled:

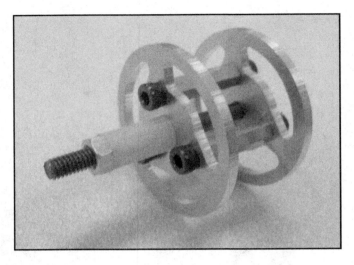

3. Half of the wheels have three holes, the other half six, although you'll only need to assemble the wheels with three. Here is the assembled wheel for the wheels with six holes:

4. Only put screws and spacers in the holes that are by the spokes. Now that you have the smooth wheels together, you'll want to put together the wheels with spokes on the outside, in order to connect to the DC motors. Here is a picture of this wheel assembled:

5. The collar, with its two set screws, will eventually connect onto the post on the DC motors. But first, you'll want to connect your wheels to the frame. Here is how you connect the first wheel:

6. You'll want to put a nut on the screw threads. When this is all connected to the body the wheel itself needs to turn freely, so you may need to loosen the screw so that this can happen. You'll put another nut on the other side of the frame so that the wheel can't come loose.

7. Now connect all six wheels without spokes to the frame in the same way. The wheels in the front are a bit different; they will have a washer on each side as the front connection to the frame is a slot that will allow you to tighten the track. Don't tighten this connection at this time as you'll need to take it out when installing the track. Here is a picture of the wheels attached to the frame:

8. Now you are going to connect the wheels with the spikes on the outside of the rim to the DC motors and to the frame. Start by connecting the DC motors to the frame using two of the small screws from the kit. Here is a picture of the screw connections:

9. Make sure that the DC motor solder connections are facing toward the bottom of the track platform. Now place the wheel on the DC motor and tighten the set screws, also shown in the preceding picture.

10. Now remove the wheel at the front of the platform, and then place the track around the three remaining wheels. The track has two inside spikes on each track that will fit between the rims of each of the wheels, including the wheels with the spikes:

11. Then replace the front wheel by also fitting the wheel into the spikes on the track, and move the wheel toward the front of the platform as far as it will go, tightening the track. Here is what it will look like when completed:

12. Now solder to wires to each of the DC motors, like this:

13. Feed these wires up to the top of the platform; you are going to connect them to a DC motor control board.

Now that the mechanical hardware is in place, you'll need to add the Raspberry Pi and a DC motor controller.

Adding the Raspberry P and a DC motor controller

You'll use the same controller you used in `Chapter 2`, *Building Your Own Futuristic Robot*. This is the **RaspiRobot Board V3**. Again, here is a picture of the board:

The board will provide the drive signals for the motors on each of the wheels. Here are the steps to connect Raspberry Pi to the board:

1. First, connect the battery power connector to the power connector on the side of the board. In this case you'll want a voltage of somewhere around 11V. A 3S RC LiPo battery will be perfect at 11.1V. Here is a picture of just such a battery:

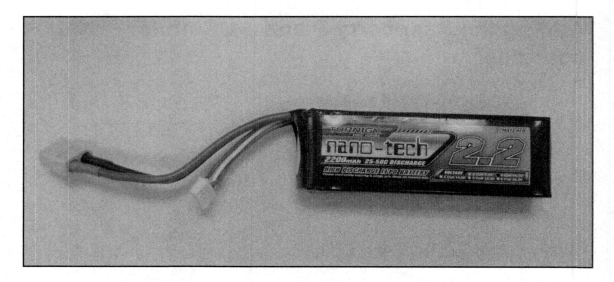

   This battery will come with two connectors, one with larger gauge wires for normal usage and a smaller connector for connecting to the battery recharger. You'll want to build connectors that can connect to the screw type connectors of the servo controller. I purchased some XT60 connector pairs and soldered some wires to the mating connector of the battery and then screwed these into the RaspiRobot Board.

2. Next, connect the two wires from the left DC motor on the tracked platform to the DC motor connectors marked L on the board.

3. Connect the other two wires from the right DC motor on the tracked platform of the other motor to the DC motor connectors marked R on the board.

Once completed, your connections should look like this:

Now you can will be able to control both the speed and the direction of the motors through the motor control board.

Now that you have the platform together you'll want to build Wall-E's arms.

Building Wall-E's arms

There are many ways to do this, but let's start with some Lynxmotion pieces that are readily available at most online robotics outlets, including eBay and Robotshop. You'll want some servo brackets and other robotics hardware.

The item on the right is a standard servo bracket, and the item on the left is an extended body bracket. You'll need seven servo brackets and one main body bracket. Here are two additional pieces you'll need:

The one on the left is a *C* servo bracket, and the item on the right is an *L* connector bracket. You'll need three *C* servo brackets, and two *L* connector brackets. You'll also need six standard size servos for this project.

 You can purchase each of these separately, but if you'd like you can buy the **17DOF Biped Robotic Educational Robot Humanoid Robot Kit Servo Bracket** on eBay, which will come with all the servo bracket parts you'll need to build your Wall-E.

You'll also need three lengths of aluminum tubing, 3 inches in length, and six Aluminum Tubing Option Connector Hubs. Here is a picture of the tubing and hub:

You'll need six standard sized servos. Here is a picture of the **Hitec HS-645MG**, a servo with excellent torque and metal gears for durability:

In addition, you'll want six metal servo horns, like the one mounted on the servo. The last two pieces you need are hands or claws for your Wall-E. In this project, I'll illustrate a hand on one arm and a claw on the other, but you can mix and match as you see fit. Here is a picture of the **Lynxmotion hand**:

This is shown with the hand constructed and the servos installed. You can use **Hitec HS-422 servos** here; they have less torque and are less expensive. And here is a picture of a robotic claw that fits a standard servo:

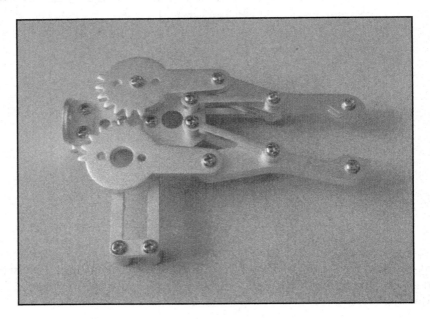

Now that you have all the parts, you can start constructing the arms and robotic hand of your Wall-E.

Constructing the arms

Here are the steps to construct the arm with the robotic hand:

1. Start by constructing the hand as instructed with the documentation that comes with the hand.

2. Then connect the a *C* bracket to a standard servo bracket like this:

3. Now connect this assembly to the hand using a bearing on the back, and connecting to the servo on the front, like this:

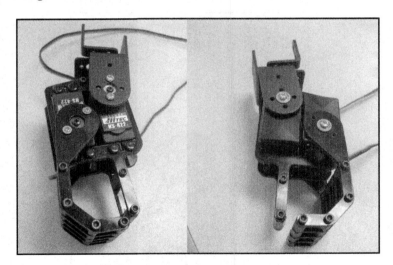

4. Connect the servo bracket to one end of a three-inch aluminum tube with hub installed, like this:

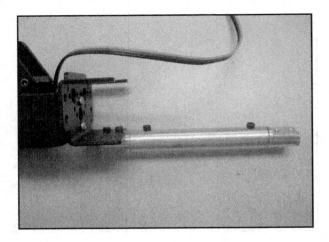

Now your arm with the hand is complete. Here is a picture of the completed assembly:

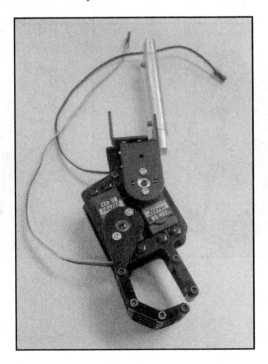

Constructing the arm with the claw is a bit different. Here is a picture of the finished assembly:

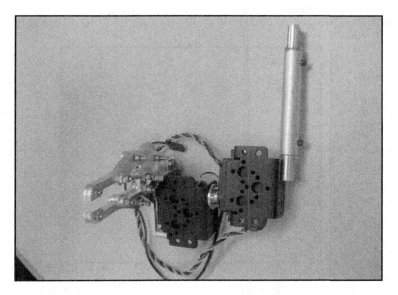

Here are the steps for constructing the claw arm:

1. You construct the arm with the claw by first connecting the aluminum tubing with the connecting hub to a servo bracket.
2. Then mount a servo in this bracket, and connect it to a servo bracket.
3. Now mount another servo and connect this servo to the claw.

You have both arms; now you'll want to connect them to the shoulder assembly and connect the entire assembly to the tracked vehicle. Here are the steps:

1. Attach an *L* bracket to each side of the elongated body bracket like this:

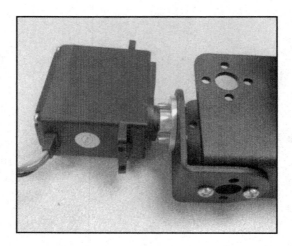

2. Do the same on the other side of the elongated body bracket.
3. Now connect the upper tubing with hub to a servo bracket like this:

4. Repeat this with the other arm and then connect these brackets to the servos on each side of the elongated body like this:

5. Now that the arm infrastructure is built, you'll need to build the base for this infrastructure. You'll do this with two C brackets and two servo brackets, all connected to the tracked base and one end of an aluminum tube, like this:

6. The next step is to connect a servo bracket to the back of the elongated base and then connect one of the connector hubs to this bracket, like this:

7. Then the final step is to feed this end connector into the open end of the aluminum tube that is connected to the tracked vehicle like this:

8. Now your hardware build is almost complete. Just place the Kinect 360 on the top of the elongated body bracket like this:

9. The last step is to build a simple yellow box around the body of your Wall-E. The easiest and least expensive way is to use yellow poster board. You can use black permanent marker to add a realistic touch to the project.

Here is a picture of the finished hardware:

Now you are ready to start controlling your Wall-E.

Controlling Wall-E's tracks using a Raspberry Pi in Python

The hardware is ready; now you can access this functionality from a Raspberry Pi. First, install the library associated with the control board, found at `http://www.monkmakes.com/rrb3/`. Perform the following steps:

1. Type `cd ~`.
2. Run the `git clone https://github.com/simonmonk/raspirobotboard3.git`—command this will retrieve the library.
3. Then type `cd raspirobotboard3/python` to go to the `raspirobotboard3/python` directory.
4. Type `sudo python setup.py install`—this will install the files.

Now you'll create some Python code that will allow you to access both the DC motors on your tracked platform. Here is some basic code that allows you to do this:

```python
#!/usr/bin/python

import time
from rrb3 import *

rr = RRB3(9, 6)
rr.set_motors(1, 0, 1, 0)
time.sleep(1)
rr.set_motors(0, 0, 0, 0)
rr.sw1_closed()
```

The lines of the code import the time and rrb3 libraries. The time library will allow you to delay your program, and the rrb3 library allows you access to the RaspiRobotBoard3. The `rr = RRB2(9,6)` line allows you to access the functionality on the RaspiRobotBoard3. `rr.set_motors(1, 0, 1, 0)` turns on both motors at full speed. `time.sleep(1)` pauses the program for 1 second. The `rr.set_motors(0, 0, 0, 0)` function stops the motors.

When you have created the code, save it under the filename `johnny.py`. Now you can run the program by typing `python johnny.py`. The tracks should move in the forward direction. This confirms that you have connected everything correctly. As in `Chapter 2`, *Building Your Own Futuristic Robot*, you may want to add dynamic control of the motors. Here is the Python code:

```python
#!/usr/bin/python

import time
from rrb3 import *
import termios
import sys
import tty

def getch():
    fd = sys.stdin.fileno()
    old_settings = termios.tcgetattr(fd)
    tty.setraw(sys.stdin.fileno())
    ch = sys.stdin.read(1)
    termios.tcsetattr(fd, termios.TCSADRAIN, old_settings)
    print '\n char is '' + ch + ''\n'
    return ch
rr = RRB3(9, 6)
var = 'n'
print "starting up"
while var != 'q':
    var = getch()
    if var == 'f':
        rr.set_motors(1, 0, 1, 0)
    if var == 'b':
        rr.set_motors(1, 1, 1, 1)
    if var == 's':
        rr.set_motors(0, 0, 0, 0)
    if var == ',':
        rr.set_motors(1, 1, 1, 0)
    if var == '.':
        rr.set_motors(1, 0, 1, 1)
rr.sw1_closed()
```

In this code, you'll have some additional import statements, termios, sys, and tty; these will allow you to sense key presses from the keyboard without hitting the *Enter* key. This will make the real-time interface seem more real-time. The getch() function senses the actual key press.

The second part of the code is a while loop that takes the input and translates it into commands for your Wall-E, moving it forward and backward and turning right and left. This program is quite simple, you'll almost certainly want to add more commands that provide more ways to control the speed and direction.

You may also want to call the Wall-E functions from another program. Instead of processing key presses, you'll want to call the program with command line arguments. Here is the Python code for that:

```
#!/usr/bin/python
import time
from rrb3 import *
import sys

rr = RRB3(9, 6)
if (sys.argv[1]) == "f":
    rr.set_motors(1, 0, 1, 0)
    time.sleep(1)
    rr.set_motors(0, 0, 0, 0)
if (sys.argv[1]) == "b":
    rr.set_motors(1, 1, 1, 1)
    time.sleep(1)
    rr.set_motors(0, 0, 0, 0)
if (sys.argv[1]) == "l":
    rr.set_motors(1, 1, 1, 0)
    time.sleep(1)
    rr.set_motors(0, 0, 0, 0)
if (sys.argv[1]) == "r":
    rr.set_motors(1, 0, 1, 1)
    time.sleep(1)
    rr.set_motors(0, 0, 0, 0)

if (sys.argv[1]) == "s":
    rr.set_motors(0, 0, 0, 0)
rr.sw1_closed()
```

Again, you may want to start with the basic johnny.py program and then add the additional capability. You'll add the import sys so that you have access to the system arguments, or the arguments you type in the command line when you type the name of the program. You'll also need to the set of if statements at the end of the program so that your robot will respond based on the command you type. Save this program under the name johnnyArg.py.

For example, if you type python ./johnnyArg.py f, Wall-E should move forward. If you type python ./johnnyArg.py b, it will move backward. There is also a way to make the robot turn left or right. Again, since #!/usr/bin/python is on the first line of the program, if you make this program executable by typing chmod +x ./johnnyArg.py, then you can run the program by simply typing ./johnnyArg.py f.

Now to controlling Wall-E's arms. You could perhaps control a single servo directly from the Raspberry Pi, but in this project you'll control six servos at the same time, so it will make more sense to use an external servo controller that can supply the control signals and supply voltages for all six servos. Since servos are the main component of this project, it is perhaps useful to go through a tutorial on servos and how to control them.

How servo motors work

Servo motors are somewhat similar to DC motors; however, there is an important difference. While DC motors are generally designed to move in a continuous way—rotating 360 degrees at a given speed—servos are generally designed to move to a limited set of angles. In other words, in the DC motor world, you generally want your motors to spin with a continuous rotation speed that you control. In the servo world, you want your motor to move to a specific position that you control. This is done by sending a **Pulse-Width-Modulated (PWM)** signal to the control connector of the servo. PWM simply means that you are going to change the length of each pulse of electrical energy in order to control something. In this case, the length of this pulse will control the angle of the servo, like this:

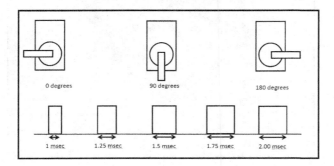

These pulses are sent out with a repetition rate of 60 Hz. You can position the servo at any angle by sending the correct control pulse.

Using a servo controller to control the servos

To make your arms move, you first need to connect the servo motor controller to the servos. The servo controller you are going to use for this project is a simple servo motor controller utilizing USB from Pololu, Pololu item #: 1354 available at `http://www.pololu.com`, which can control 18 servo motors.

Here is a picture of the unit:

Make sure you order the assembled version. This piece of hardware will turn USB commands from the Raspberry Pi Zero into signals that control your servo motors. Pololu makes a number of different versions of this controller, each able to control a certain number of servos. In this case, you may want to choose the 18-servo version so you can control all 12 servos with one controller and also add an additional servo to control the direction of a camera or sensor. You could also choose the 12-servo version. One advantage of the 18-servo controller is the ease of connecting power to the unit via screw connectors.

There are two connections you'll need to make to the servo controller to get started; the first is to the servo motors, the second to a battery. So first, connect the servos to the controller. In order to be consistent, let's connect your six servos to the connections marked 0 through 5 on the controller using this configuration:

Servo connector	Servo
0	Claw Gripper Open/Close
1	Claw Gripper Up/Down
2	Claw Arm Up/Down
3	Hand Arm Up/Down
4	Hand Back/Forth
5	Hand Open/Close

Here is a picture of the back of the controller; this will tell us where to connect our servos:

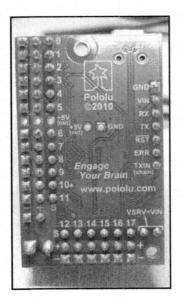

Now you need to connect the servo motor controller to your battery. You'll need around 6 to 7V to power the servo motor controller. There are two ways to get this. The first is use a 2S RC LiPo battery. The 2S means that the battery will have two cells, with an output voltage of 7.2V. It will supply the voltage and current needed by your servos, which can be of the order of 2A.

You can also use the 11.1V 3S battery that you are using to power the DC motors that run the tracks, however you'll need a voltage regulator to change this voltage down to the voltage for the servos.

Here is a picture of such a regulator:

These are available at most electronics online stores. Some are quite simple; this one actually has a display so you can adjust it to the desired output voltage. You connect your 3S battery to one side, the servo controller to the other, then adjust the voltage to the desired level.

Now that you have connected your servo controller to power, you'll connect the motor controller to your personal computer to check to see if you can communicate with it. To do this, connect a mini USB cable between the servo controller and your personal computer. I'll detail the directions with a PC, but you can also do this step with a Mac or Linux. Those details are on the website at https://www.pololu.com/docs/J4.

Communicating between the servo controller and a PC

Now that the servo controller is connected ,you can use some software provided by Pololu to control the servos. This is done just to make sure you have everything hooked up correctly, and to set the controller's setting. Unfortunately, the software won't run on the Raspberry Pi; you'll need to do this using your personal computer. First, download the Pololu Software from `www.pololu.com/docs/0J40/3.a` and install it according to the instructions on the website.

Once it is installed, run the software, and you should see this screen:

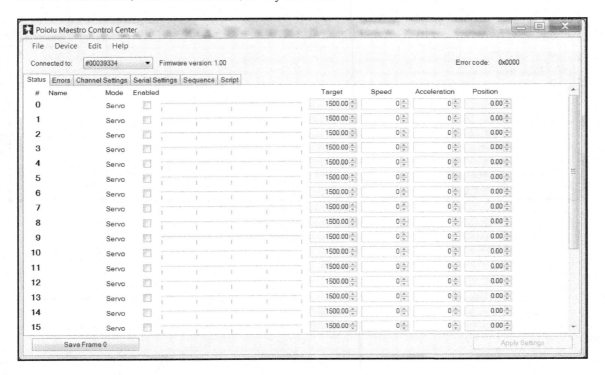

You will first need to change the configuration on **Serial Settings**, so select the **Serial Settings** tab, and you should see this:

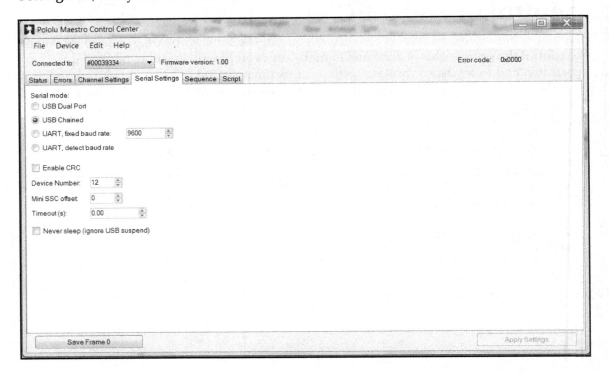

Make sure that the **USB Chained** is selected; this will allow you to connect and control the motor controller over USB. Now go back to the main screen by selecting the **Status** tab, and now you can actually turn on the 12 servos. The screen should look like this:

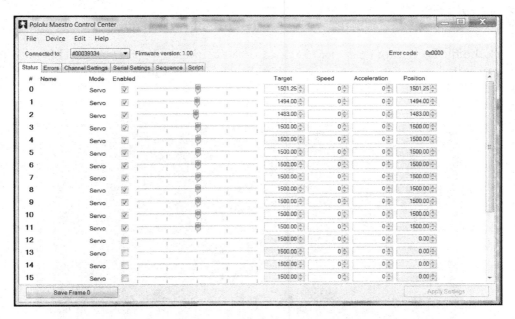

Now you can use the sliders to actually control the servos. Make sure that servo 0 moves the claw open/closed servo, the claw rotate servo, and so on. You can also use this to position the servos. For servos connected to the claw and hand, set all of the servos so that the slider is in the middle. Now unscrew the servo horn on each servo until the servos are centered at this location. For the two servos at the shoulder, you'll want them to be straight down when the servo is at 50 or 130 degrees, respectively, depending on which side the servo is on.

Controlling the Servo Controller with the Raspberry Pi

You've checked the servo motor controller, and the servos, you'll now connect the motor controller up to the Raspberry Pi and make sure you can control the servos from it. Remove the USB cable from the PC and connect it to the Raspberry Pi.

Let's now talk to the motor controller by downloading the Linux code from Pololu at `www.pololu.com/docs/0J40/3.b`. Perhaps the best way is to log onto your Raspberry Pi Zero with putty, then type `wget` to get the latest download from the site. Then move the file using `mv maestro-linux-******.tar.gz\?file_id\=0J315 maestro-linux-******.tar.gz`, where `*******` is the current version number of the file.

Unpack the file by typing `tar -xzfv maestro-linux-******.tar.gz`. This will create a directory called `maestro_linux`. Go to that directory by typing `cd maestro_linux`, and then type `ls -l`. You should see something like this:

```
pi@raspberrypi: ~/maestro-linux
pi@raspberrypi:~/maestro-linux $ ls -l
total 324
-rw-r--r-- 1 pi pi     55 Jan 16  2015 99-pololu.rules
-rw-r--r-- 1 pi pi  19968 Jan 16  2015 Bytecode.dll
-rw-r--r-- 1 pi pi  29696 Jan 16  2015 FirmwareUpgrade.dll
-rwxr-xr-x 1 pi pi 183296 Jan 16  2015 MaestroControlCenter
-rw-r--r-- 1 pi pi   1483 Jan 16  2015 README.txt
-rw-r--r-- 1 pi pi  11264 Jan 16  2015 Sequencer.dll
-rw-r--r-- 1 pi pi  12800 Jan 16  2015 UsbWrapper.dll
-rwxr-xr-x 1 pi pi  15872 Jan 16  2015 UscCmd
-rw-r--r-- 1 pi pi  38400 Jan 16  2015 Usc.dll
pi@raspberrypi:~/maestro-linux $ []
```

The **README.txt** document will give you explicit instructions on how to install the software. This basically is done in two steps:

1. First, install a set of supporting libraries by typing:
   `sudo apt-get install libusb-1.0-0-dev mono-runtime libmono-winforms2.0-cil`.
2. Then copy the configuration file by typing:
   `sudo cp 99-pololu.rules /etc/udev/rules.d/`.

As noted earlier in the chapter, you can't run `MaestroControlCenter` on your Raspberry Pi, but you can control your servos using the `UscCmd` command-line application to test that they are connected and working correctly.

First, type ./UscCmd --list, and you should see the following:

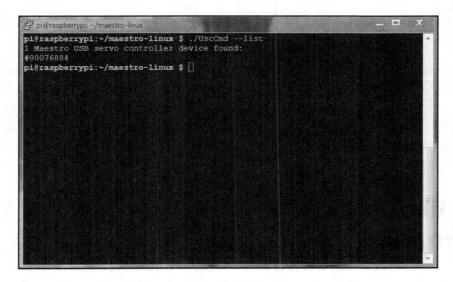

The unit sees our servo controller. If you just type ./UscCmd, you can see all the commands you could send to your controller:

Notice you can send a servo a specific target angle, although the target is not in degrees of angle values so it makes it a bit difficult to know where you are sending your servo. Try typing ./UscCmd --servo 0, 10. The servo will move to its full angle position. Type ./UscCmd - servo 0, 0, which will stop the servo from trying to move.

In the next section, you'll write some Python code that will translate your angles to the commands that the servo controller will want to see to move it to specific angle locations.

 If you didn't run the Windows version of Maestro Controller and set the Serial Settings to USB Chained, your motor controller may not respond. Rerun the `MaestroController` code and set the Serial Settings to USB Chained.

Creating a program in Linux to control Wall-E's arms

You now know that you can talk to your servo motor controller, and move your servos. In this section you'll create a Python program that will let you talk to your servos to move them to specific angles.

Let's start with a simple program that will set Wall-E's arms to an initial position. To access the serial port, you'll need to make sure you have the Python serial library. Type sudo apt-get install python-serial.

Now you'll want to enter your program. Here is the code:

```python
#!/usr/bin/python
import serial
import time

def setAngle(ser, channel, angle):
    minAngle = 0.0
    maxAngle = 180.0
    minTarget = 256.0
    maxTarget = 13120.0
    scaledValue = int((angle/((maxAngle - minAngle) / (maxTarget -
minTarget))) + minTarget)
    commandByte = chr(0x84)
    channelByte = chr(channel)
    lowTargetByte = chr(scaledValue & 0x7F)
    highTargetByte = chr(scaledValue >> 7) & 0x7F)
    command = commandByte + channelByte + lowTargetByte + highTargetByte
    ser.write(command)
```

```
        ser.flush()

ser = serial.Serial("/dev/ttyACM0", 9600)

setAngle(ser,  0,  90)
setAngle(ser,  1,  90)
setAngle(ser,  2,  50)
setAngle(ser,  3,  140)
setAngle(ser,  4,  0)
setAngle(ser,  5,  0)
time.sleep(1)
```

This particular controller uses two bytes of information, so the code in the `setAngle` function will translate the input of the channel and angle to numbers that the controller can understand. For more specifics, see `http://www.pololu.com/docs/J4`.

Here is an explanation of the code:

- `#! /usr/bin/python`: This first line allows you to make this Python file execute from the command line.
- `import serial`: This line imports the serial library. You need the serial library to talk to your unit via USB.
- `import time`: This line imports the time library, allowing you to issue the `time.sleep(1)` command, which pauses the program for 1 second.
- `def setAngle(ser, channel, angle)`: This function converts your desired setting of servo and angle into the serial command that the servo motor controller needs.
- `setAngle(ser, [servo], [angle])`: Now you can set each servo to the home position.

After you have installed the serial library, you can run your program by typing `sudo python walleArms.py`. You can now ask your robot to position its arm by running this program and typing the in the position of the servos, such as the capability shown in the Python program to control the DC motors that control the tracks. Here is that code:

```
#!/usr/bin/python
import serial
import time

def setAngle(ser, channel, angle):
    minAngle = 0.0
    maxAngle = 180.0
    minTarget = 256.0
    maxTarget = 13120.0
```

```
        scaledValue = int((angle / ((maxAngle - minAngle) / (maxTarget -
minTarget))\
) + minTarget)
    commandByte = chr(0x84)
    channelByte = chr(channel)
    lowTargetByte = chr(scaledValue & 0x7F)
    highTargetByte = chr((scaledValue >> 7) & 0x7F)
    command = commandByte + channelByte + lowTargetByte + highTargetByte
    ser.write(command)
    ser.flush()

ser = serial.Serial("/dev/ttyACM0", 9600)
servo = 0
angle = 0

while(servo != 10):
    servo = int(raw_input("Servo: "))
    angle = int(raw_input("Angle: "))
    setAngle(ser, servo, angle)
```

Using the program, you can position the arms any way you like. The best way to learn is to try new and different positions with the servos. Here is an example of running the program:

Now you'll want to add the Kinect 360 to your Wall-E.

Adding the Kinect 360 to your Wall-E

Now that you can move around you should add a way for your Wall-E to see so that it won't run into walls. To do this, you'll use a Kinect 360, an amazing device from Microsoft that will not only give you a picture but also a depth image of your surroundings.

The Kinect 360 is particularly interesting because it provides all this in one package, and has a set of libraries that support the entire process. First, you'll need to connect the Kinect to the Raspberry Pi 3. This is a little difficult because the power and USB connections on the Kinect 360 are designed to connect to the Xbox 360 and a standard power outlet. So you'll need to do some modifications to the wires.

The Kinect 360 plugs into a connector that provides a USB connector that connects to the Raspberry Pi. That's the easy part. This connection also plugs into a standard wall socket. You'll need to cut the cable that comes out of the wall socket transformer/adapter and expose the wires, like this:

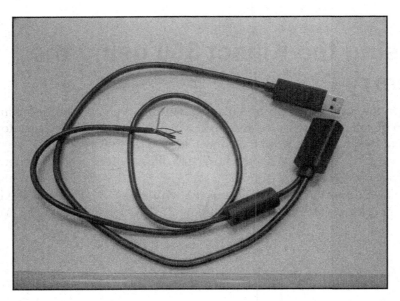

There are two wires, a white and brown wire; they look like this:

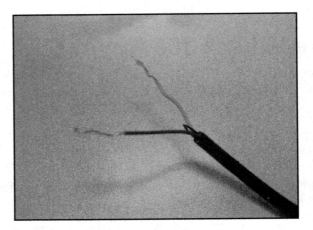

The brown wire is the ground wire; you'll connect that to the ground wire on your 3S LiPo battery. The brown wires you'll connect to the 11.1V connection on your battery so that your Kinect can work remotely.

Accessing the Kinect 360 using the Raspberry Pi

Once you have the unit connected and up and working, you can access the images. First, you'll need to install a library called **freenect**, which will make it very easy to access both the regular and depth images from the Kinect 360. To do this, type `sudo apt-get install freenect`. You'll also need a library to allow you to access freenect from Python; to get this, type `sudo apt-get install python-freenect`. Once you have the libraries installed, you'll also need to install a library that will allow you to access the images on the Raspberry Pi graphics system. To do this, type `sudo apt-get install libgl1-mesa-swx11`.

You can check to see if everything is working by opening a vncserver window and typing `freenect-glview`. You should see something like this:

This shows both the depth and regular image. The depth image is color coded: white is closer, then red, then yellow, then green.

This is neat, but you'll want to access both images using OpenCV just like you did in `Chapter 2`, *Building Your Own Futuristic Robot*. If you don't have OpenCV installed, follow the instructions there to install it. Once it's installed, you can make sure it is working properly by running the `camera.py` demonstration program in `/home/pi/examples/python`. Accessing the regular image using the freenect library is quite simple. Here is some code:

```
#import the necessary modules
import freenect
import cv2

while True:
    array,_ = freenect.sync_get_video()
    array = cv2.cvtColor(array,cv2.COLOR_RGB2BGR)
    cv2.imshow('RGB image',array)
    if cv2.waitKey(10) == 27:
        break
cv2.destroyAllWindows()
```

The first few lines import the libraries that you'll need, such as freenect, to get data from the Kinect 360. OpenCV capability is available when you import cv2. The while loop gets the video from the freenect library, converts it to an RGB image, and then displays the image.

When you run this program you should see the regular image, like this:

But you also want to access the depth camera. Here is the code that shows you how to access the depth map:

```
import freenect
import cv2
import numpy as np

while True:
    depth, timestamp = freenect.sync_get_depth()
    np.clip(depth, 0, 2**10 - 1, depth)
    depth >>= 2
    depth = depth.astype(np.uint8)
    blur = cv2.GaussianBlur(depth, (5, 5), 0)
    cv2.imshow('image', blur)
    if cv2.waitKey(10) == 27:
        break

cv2.destroyAllWindows()
```

This code is quite simple. NumPy is library that provides matrix operations. The program loops them through until the *Esc* key is pressed, gets the image, clips the image to the depth, reduces the noise in the image using a `GaussianBlur` function, and then displays the image. When you run the program you should see something like this:

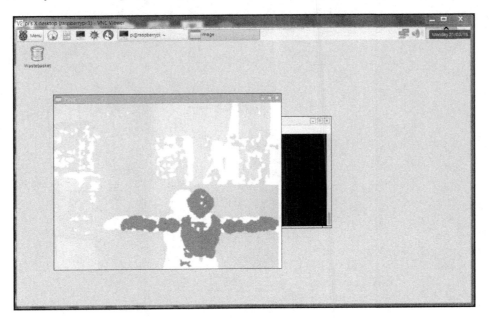

In this screenshot, each image will express a value in color, but also in depth. Now that you have access to both depth and video images you can use the advanced features of OpenCV to find motion or color to find objects or barriers.

Controlling your Wall-E remotely

As in Chapter 2, *Building Your Own Futuristic Robot*, now you can have access, via vncserver, to a video feed or a depth image, and control the arms and tracks of your robot. Simply access vncserver, open a Terminal window, and run the desired programs. Now you can remotely control Wall-E using a host computer, tablet, or even cell phone.

Summary

Now you have your own Wall-E robot that can run autonomously or be controlled remotely. You could also use the principles described in Chapter 2, *Building Your Own Futuristic Robot,* to add the ability to respond to voice commands. You've now mastered these two projects that let you explore on land. Your next project will be a fish so that you can explore underwater.

4

Building a Robotic Fish

Now you've built an R2D2 and a Wall-E robot. Let's turn your attention to the great deep. Let's build a robot that can swim in water. This will use your knowledge of how to control servos, and you'll want a webcam to see what your fish is seeing, but this project can't be controlled using a wireless connection, as that doesn't work well in water. So you'll control your fish using a LAN cable so that you can control your fish from the surface.

In this chapter, we'll cover these topics:

- Creating a swimming robot using servos and Raspberry Pi
- Connecting an IMU unit to help the robot stay upright, and also a compass to know which direction the robot fish is going

Since it is much more difficult to buy an existing toy to use as a platform, you will be creating your own model of robotic fish. You can either use a 3D printed model or use acrylic to cut your own. This will provide the basic swimming mechanism; the rest is up to you.

Creating the hardware platform

There are two possible ways to create the plastic shell of your swimming robot. One is to use a 3D printer to print a simple model. Here is a link to such a fish robot:
`http://www.thingiverse.com/thing:3539`.

Or you can waterproof a standard servo. `http://www.societyofrobots.com/actuators_w aterproof_servo.shtml` is a link to some instructions on various methods. Either way, you'll use standard servo brackets to build the tail. Start by using a standard servo bracket and attaching an *L* bracket to it, like this:

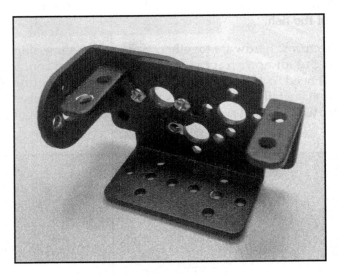

Eventually, you'll connect the other side of this *L* bracket to the body of the fish. Now you can mount your waterproof servo into the bracket, and also connect a servo horn to the servo, like this:

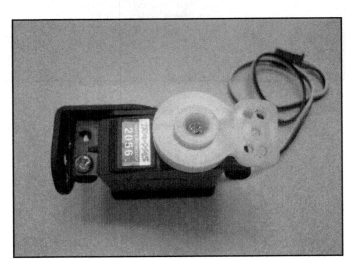

Now connect to *L* brackets together. These will eventually connect the servo to the tail. Here is this connection:

Now connect this structure to the waterproof servo via the servo horn, like this:

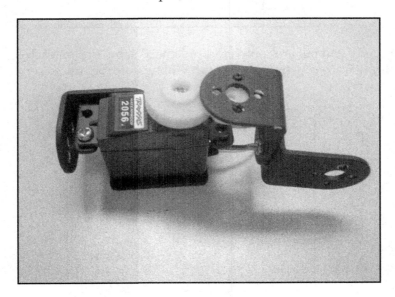

Now drill some holes in the tail piece and connect the plastic tail to the structure. Here is a look at the constructed tail:

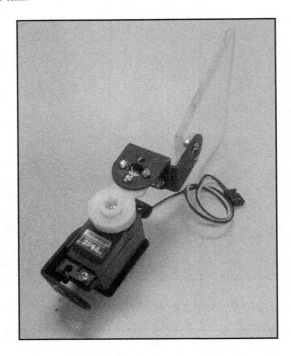

Now that your body and tail are complete, you'll need some fins on each side to control the direction of your fish. To construct these, start with waterproof micro servos. Here is an image of such a servo:

As with the case of standard waterproof servos, you can also choose to waterproof a standard micro servo. But first you'll want to connect the micro servo bracket to the body of the fish, like this:

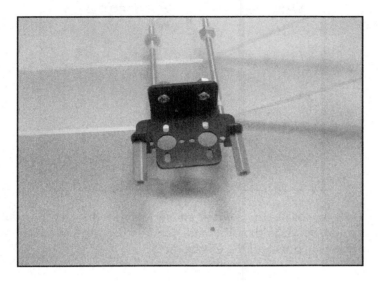

Next, you'll connect your servo to a micro servo bracket, like this:

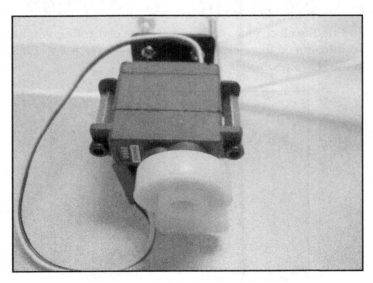

Now connect the servo horn to an *L* bracket and a fin, like this:

Notice that the front edge of the fin is cut at an angle to cut through the water easier. Connect a second micro servo to the other side, and now your fish has all the mechanical parts in place. Now let's connect all the electronics.

Adding the electronics to your fish

The first step in adding the electronics is to add a servo controller; you'll use the same controller that was introduced in `Chapter 3`, *Building a Wall-E Robot*. First, you'll hook the three servos up to the servo controller, like this:

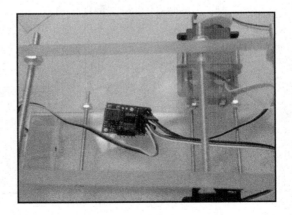

Now you can connect the servo controller to the battery. This is a bit complicated, as you'll need to connect the battery to the servo controller and to the Raspberry Pi. For the connection to the Raspberry Pi, you'll want to use a voltage regulator to convert your LiPo battery voltage to the 5V required by the Raspberry Pi. Here is an image of such a regulator:

These are available at most online electronics retailers. And you'll want to make sure you have a power switch so that you can turn your entire system on and off. These are also available at most online electronics retailers. Here is a diagram of the entire power system:

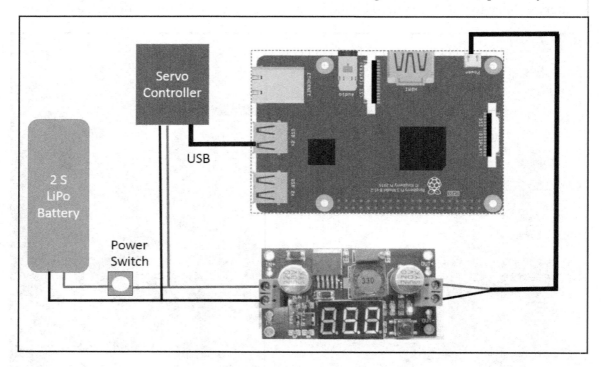

Once you have the servo controller connected to the servos and battery, you'll want to connect the USB port to your PC and access the servos using the Pololu Maestro Control Center Software as described in Chapter 3, *Building a Wall-E Robot*. You can test the servos and configure the servo controller. Once you've been able to exercise the servos, install the Maestro control software onto the Raspberry Pi, as described in the Chapter 3, *Building a Wall-E Robot*.

Accessing the servos through software is quite simple. Here is some code to do that:

```python
#!/usr/bin/python
import serial
import time

def setSpeed(ser, channel,speed):
    if speed > 127 or speed <0:
        speed=1
    commandByte = chr(0x87)
    channelByte = chr(channel)
    highByte, lowByte = divmod(speed,32)
    highTargetByte = chr(highByte)
    lowTargetByte = chr(lowByte << 2)
    command = commandByte + channelByte + lowTargetByte + highTargetByte
    ser.write(command)
    ser.flush()

def setAngle(ser, channel, angle):
    minAngle = 0.0
    maxAngle = 180.0
    minTarget = 256.0
    maxTarget = 13120.0
    scaledValue = int((angle/((maxAngle - minAngle) / (maxTarget -
minTarget))) + minTarget)
    commandByte = chr(0x84)
    channelByte = chr(channel)
    lowTargetByte = chr(scaledValue & 0x7F)
    highTargetByte = chr((scaledValue >> 7) & 0x7F)
    command = commandByte + channelByte + lowTargetByte + highTargetByte
    ser.write(command)
    ser.flush()

ser = serial.Serial("/dev/ttyACM0", 9600)
setAngle(ser, 0, 90)
setAngle(ser, 1, 90)
setAngle(ser, 2, 90)
time.sleep(1)

servo = 0
angle = 0
speed = 1
while(servo != 10):
    servo = int(raw_input("Servo: "))
    angle = int(raw_input("Angle: "))
    speed = int(raw_input("Speed: "))
    setSpeed(ser, servo, speed)
    setAngle(ser, servo, angle)
```

If you run this program, you can control each of the servos individually. But you might want to create a command interface so that a single character makes the tail go back and forth, another command positions the front fins so that your fish goes up, another so that your fish goes down, another so that your fish swims to the right, and yet another so that your fish turns to the left. Here is some code that accomplishes this:

```python
#!/usr/bin/python
import serial
import time
import sys
import tty
import termios

def setSpeed(ser, channel,speed):
    if speed > 127 or speed <0:
        speed=1
    commandByte = chr(0x87)
    channelByte = chr(channel)
    highByte, lowByte = divmod(speed,32)
    highTargetByte = chr(highByte)
    lowTargetByte = chr(lowByte << 2)
    command = commandByte + channelByte + lowTargetByte + highTargetByte
    ser.write(command)
    ser.flush()

def setAngle(ser, channel, angle):
    minAngle = 0.0
    maxAngle = 180.0
    minTarget = 256.0
    maxTarget = 13120.0
    scaledValue = int((angle/((maxAngle - minAngle) / (maxTarget -
minTarget))) + minTarget)
    commandByte = chr(0x84)
    channelByte = chr(channel)
    lowTargetByte = chr(scaledValue & 0x7F)
    highTargetByte = chr((scaledValue >> 7) & 0x7F)
    command = commandByte + channelByte + lowTargetByte + highTargetByte
    ser.write(command)
    ser.flush()

def getch():
    fd = sys.stdin.fileno()
    old_settings = termios.tcgetattr(fd)
    tty.setraw(sys.stdin.fileno())
    ch = sys.stdin.read(1)
    termios.tcsetattr(fd, termios.TCSADRAIN, old_settings)
    return ch
```

```
ser = serial.Serial("/dev/ttyACM0", 9600)
setAngle(ser, 0, 90)
setAngle(ser, 1, 90)
setAngle(ser, 2, 90)
time.sleep(1)

speed = 20
var = 'n'
print "starting up"
while var != 'q':
    var = getch()
    if var == 'f':
        setSpeed(ser, 2, 20)
        setAngle(ser, 2, 70)
        time.sleep(.5)
        setAngle(ser, 2, 110)
        time.sleep(.5)
        setAngle(ser, 2, 90)
    if var == 'd':
        setSpeed(ser, 0, 20)
        setAngle(ser, 0, 100)
        setSpeed(ser, 1, 20)
        setAngle(ser, 1, 80)
    if var == 'u':
        setSpeed(ser, 0, 20)
        setAngle(ser, 0, 80)
        setSpeed(ser, 1, 20)
        setAngle(ser, 1, 100)
    if var == 's':
        setSpeed(ser, 0, 20)
        setAngle(ser, 0, 90)
        setSpeed(ser, 1, 20)
        setAngle(ser, 1, 90)
    if var == 'r':
        setSpeed(ser, 2, 20)
        setAngle(ser, 2, 70)
        time.sleep(.5)
        setAngle(ser, 2, 90)
        time.sleep(.5)
    if var == 'l':
        setSpeed(ser, 2, 20)
        setAngle(ser, 2, 110)
        time.sleep(.5)
        setAngle(ser, 2, 90)
        time.sleep(.5)
```

When you run this program, you can press *f* and your fish will swim forward, *u* will cause the fish to go up, *d* will cause the fish to go down, *s* will level the fish, *r* will cause the fish to swim to the right, and ' will cause the fish to swim to the left. Now your fish is functional, but you'll want to add the capability to *see* what your fish is doing under the water. To do this, you'll want to add a camera, in this case, the RaspiCamera.

Adding the RaspiCamera

There is a simple yet small way to capture images and video that is perfect for this application, the Raspberry Pi camera board. Here is an image of this product:

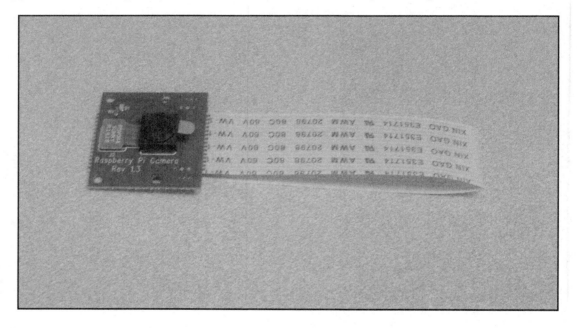

The camera connects to the Raspberry Pi by installing it into the connector marked camera on the Raspberry Pi. To see how this is done, watch the video at
`http://www.raspberrypi.org/help/camera-module-setup/`.

Once the device is connected, you can access the device by enabling it through the configuration utility. To enable the camera, perform the following steps:

1. Run the configuration utility by typing `sudo raspi-config`.

2. Select the **Enable Camera** option, as shown in the following screenshot:

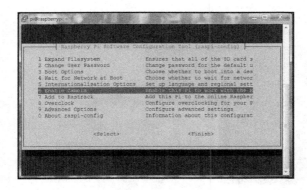

3. Select the **Enable Camera**, then exit the utility and reboot the device.

To take a picture with the camera, simply type `raspistill -o image.jpg`. This will take a picture with the camera, and then store the image in a `image.jpg` file. Once you have the picture, you can view it by opening the Raspberry Pi image viewer by selecting the lower left icon for **applications**, then **accessories**, and then **image viewer**.

Open the `image.jpg` file, and you should see the result, as shown in the following screenshot:

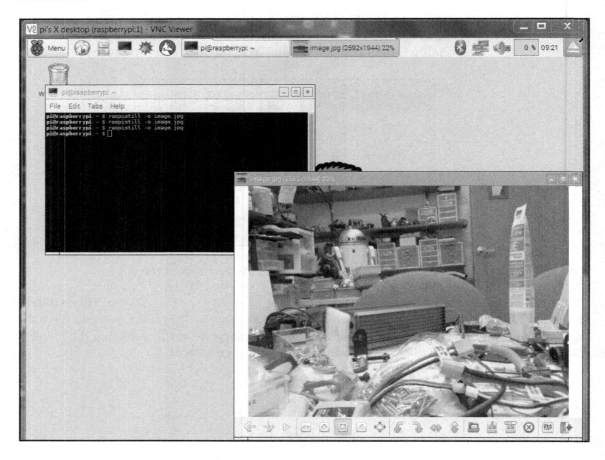

You'll also need an application to access the video feed. For RaspiCam, you can use `luvcview`. You install `luvcview` by typing `sudo apt-get install luvcview`. Once you have installed the application, you can run it by typing `luvcview`, and you should see something like this:

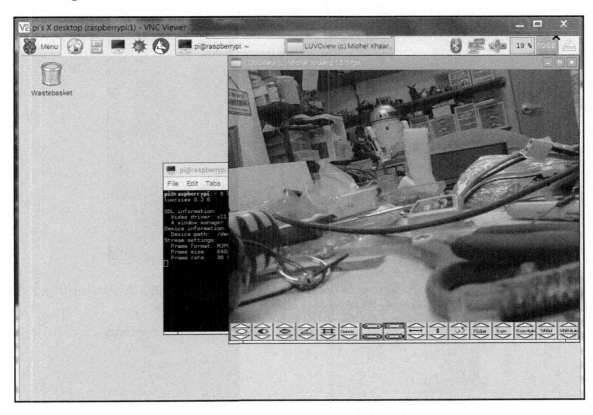

Now you'll need to mount the camera to the front of the fish. You'll want to drill small holes in the small acrylic piece that is the part of the front of the fish that points down. Now mount the camera against the acrylic, like this:

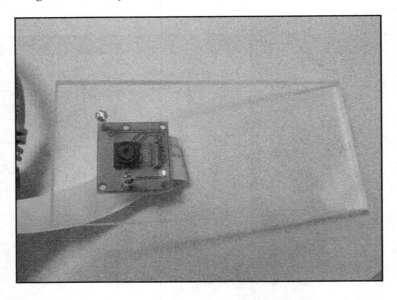

This will mount in the bottom front of your fish; you'll be looking slightly down at the underwater world. Here is how it will look in the front of the fish:

Now your electronics are all connected. Before you glue everything shut, you have one more connection to make: your LAN connection.

Controlling your fish remotely

You can, via vncserver, access the video feed and control the servos on your fish. However, you won't be able to access your fish underwater using a wireless connection. You'll need a wired LAN cable, which will represent a bit of a challenge. First, purchase an adapter that can provide a waterproof seal for the LAN cable. These are available as Black Plastic PG16 Waterproof Cable Connectors at many online retailers. Here is an image of such a device:

You'll need to drill a hole in the top of your fish, toward the back, and mount this connector. You can then feed your LAN cable through this connector and connect one end to the Raspberry Pi on your fish, and the other end to your host computer. This will allow you to both control your fish and view the video. You'll need a long length of LAN cable, preferably mounted to a reel, like this:

Now you can place all of the electronics in your fish and seal it. You'll want to make sure you put the charging port for your battery outside the fish. Simply run the charging cable on the battery through one of the seams where two pieces of the acrylic come together, like this:

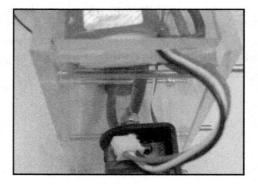

Then use the silicon glue to seal the edge. You'll also need to determine how much weight to add to make sure your fish is neutrally buoyant.

 Neutrally buoyant simply means that your fish neither sinks nor pops to the surface, but that the weight of the robot offsets the buoyancy of the air captured in your robot.

To achieve this, you can add weight after you seal your fish by screwing lead weights to the bottom, like this:

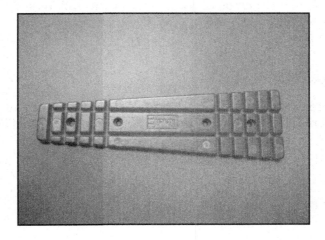

This lead weight is available at many online shops as Cub Scout Pinewood derby car weights.

You'll want to liberally use a silicon glue that can both glue the parts and make them waterproof and airtight. These are available at most home improvement stores. Apply it to all the places where your acrylic pieces meet, but also cover your screw heads and around the nuts as well. Here is an image of the whole fish:

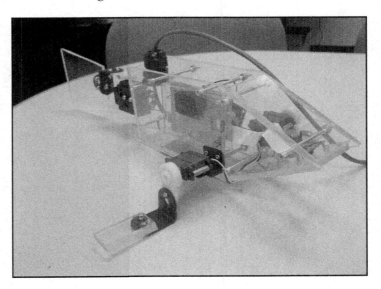

That's it. Your fish is ready for its first swim. To control your fish, simply remote in using putty and the vncviewer, run `luvcview` to see what your fish is seeing, and run your control program to send commands to your fish to swim straight, to the right or left, or up or down.

Summary

You can now explore the underwater world with your fish robot. Your next robot will offer a completely different set of challenges. You'll be building a robot hand that can move along with your hand.

5
Creating a Robotic Hand with the Raspberry Pi

Now that you are becoming something of an expert at building amazing projects with the Raspberry Pi, this project will provide you with the knowledge to begin to build your own humanoid robot. You'll start with perhaps the most interesting body part; the hand.

To do this, you will learn the following things:

- How to use Raspberry Pi to control servos that will control a robotic hand
- How to add a USB webcam to the project to sense your hand
- How to use **OpenCV(Open Source Computer Vision)**, an open source image processing library, to determine the position of your hand, and then move the robotic hand accordingly

Creating the hardware platform

In this chapter, you'll build a human hand that has four fingers, a thumb, and a rotating wrist. There are actually several possible robotic hand configurations that you can purchase or build yourself. If you'd like to purchase an already 3D printed hand, my personal favorite is the hand that was designed by Christopher Chappelle and Easton LaChappelle available already 3D printed at
http://www.shapeways.com/product/Z5CZ2RKLY/3d-printed-hand-right?li=search-results-1&optionId=42512474.

Here is an image of the hand:

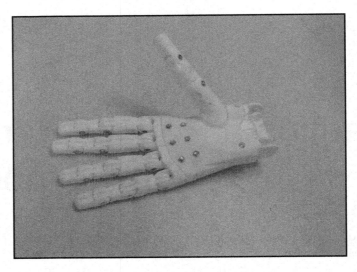

If you have access to a 3D printer, you can also download and print the hand yourself. Here is the link: `https://www.thingiverse.com/thing:288856`. Assembling the hand is quite simple; follow the instructions at `http://www.shapeways.com/product/Z5CZ2RKLY/3d-pr inted-hand-right` in the instruction image. Once you have assembled the hand, you'll need to add the servos to control the hand and the wrist. To control the hand, you'll need to pull on five separate fishing lines that come out of the hand. Here is an image of those fishing lines:

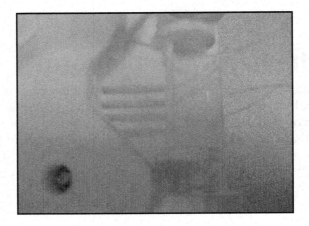

The hand is normally fully open. When you pull on the lines, each of the digits of the hand closes. When you release the lines, rubber bands on the back of each joint force the fingers and thumb back open. You use the servos to control the fingers and thumb. For this project, you'll control the fingers and thumb to mirror the position of your own hand.

Here is an image of how to connect the fishing lines to a servo:

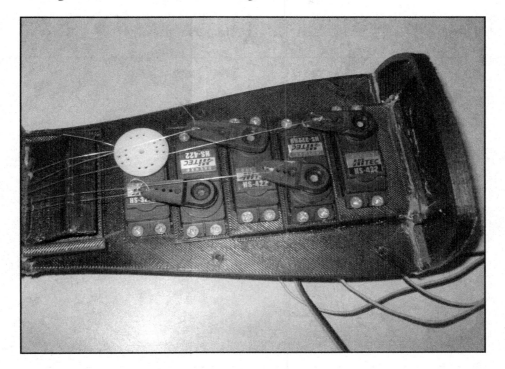

Connect each of the digits to a servo. Then connect the entire hand to a bracket; this will act as the wrist. You'll also need to connect this to a servo that can turn the wrist.

Moving the hand

In order to move the servos, you can use a servo controller similar to the one introduced in Chapter 3, *Building a Wall-E Robot*, to control six servos that will control these fingers, thumb, and wrist. As in Chapter 3, *Building a Wall-E Robot*, the servo controller you are going to use for this project is a simple servo motor controller utilizing USB from Pololu. Since you only need to control five servos, you can order the six servo controller version available at http://www.pololu.com.Here is an image of the unit:

Make sure you order the assembled version. This piece of hardware will turn USB commands from the Raspberry Pi into signals that control your servo motors. There are two connections that you'll need to make to the servo controller to get started; the first to the servo motors, the second to a power source.

First, connect the servos to the controller. In order to be consistent, let's connect your six servos to the connections marked 0 through 5 on the controller using this configuration:

Servo connector	Servo
0	Thumb
1	Index finger
2	Middle finger
3	Ring finger
4	Pinkie
5	Wrist

Here is an image of the back of the controller; this will tell us where to connect our servos:

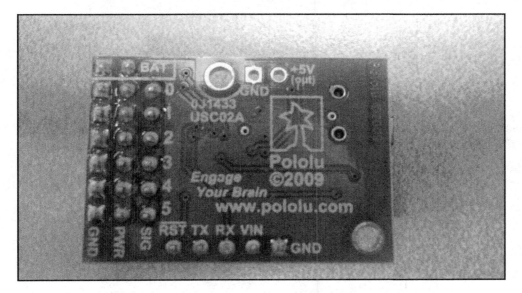

On the servo, **GND** is the black wire, **PWR** is the red wire, and **SIG** is the yellow wire. Now you need to connect the servo motor controller to a power source. For this project, you can use a battery, but you can also use a dedicated power supply. Here is an image of a dedicated power supply, available at most online electronics outlets that can provide the approximately 3 amps at 6V you'll need for the project:

The connections on the power supply are clearly marked. You'll connect the power supply 6V and **GND** connections to the connections marked **BAT** on the servo controller.

Here is an image of the connections on the servo controller:

Your system is now functional. Now you'll connect the motor controller to your personal computer to check to see if you can communicate with it as shown in `Chapter 3`, *Building a Wall-E Robot*. To do this, connect a mini USB cable between the servo controller and your personal computer.

Now you can use the sliders on the Pololu Maestro Control Center to actually control the servos. Make sure that the servo 0 control moves the thumb, servo 1 the index finger front middle servo, servo 2 the right front upper servo, and so on. You can also use this to calibrate the servos. This is how the Maestro Control Center looks, for reference:

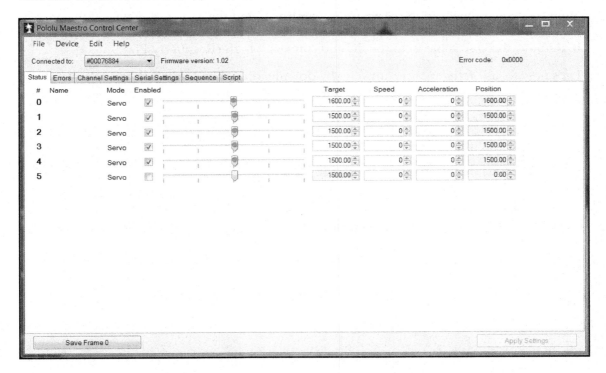

Set all of the servos so that the slider is on one side of the slider bar, as you will want this to be the open setting. Moving the slider bar to the other side will pull the fishing line, and thus the associated finger or thumb, to the closed setting. You can center your servos by unscrewing the servo horn on each servo until the servos are positioned so that the open hand is at one end of the servo movement. When the servos move to the other end of the range, the hand should close.

Your hand is now ready to actually do something. Now you'll need to send the servos the electronic signals that they need to allow the robotic hand to follow the position of your hand.

Connecting the servo controller to the Raspberry Pi

Now that you've checked the servo motor controller and the servos, you'll need to connect the servo controller up to the Raspberry Pi and make sure you can control the servos from it. Remove the USB cable from the PC and connect it to the Raspberry Pi.

Let's now focus on the motor controller by downloading the Linux code from Pololu at `www.pololu.com/docs/0J40/3.b`. Here are the steps to do so:

1. First, log on to your Raspberry Pi by putty, then type `wget.http://www.pololu.com/file/download/maestro-linux-100507.tar.gz?file_id=0J315`.
2. Move the file using `mv maestro-linux-100507.tar.gz\?file_id\=0J315 maestro-linux-100507.tar.gz`.
3. Unpack the file by typing `tar -xzfv maestro-linux-100507.tar.gz`. This will create a directory called `maestro_linux`.

4. Go to that directory by typing `cd maestro_linux` and then `ls -l`; you should see something like this:

```
pi@raspberrypi: ~/maestro_linux
pi@raspberrypi:~/maestro_linux$ ls -l
total 296
-rw-r--r-- 1 pi pi     55 May  7  2010 99-pololu.rules
-rw-r--r-- 1 pi pi  20480 May  7  2010 Bytecode.dll
-rw-r--r-- 1 pi pi  28672 May  7  2010 FirmwareUpgrade.dll
-rwxr-xr-x 1 pi pi 156160 May  7  2010 MaestroControlCenter
-rw-r--r-- 1 pi pi   4281 May  7  2010 README.txt
-rw-r--r-- 1 pi pi  11264 May  7  2010 Sequencer.dll
-rw-r--r-- 1 pi pi  12288 May  7  2010 UsbWrapper.dll
-rwxr-xr-x 1 pi pi  16384 May  7  2010 UscCmd
-rw-r--r-- 1 pi pi  37376 May  7  2010 Usc.dll
pi@raspberrypi:~/maestro_linux$ []
```

The `README.txt` file will give you explicit instructions on how to install the software. This is basically done in two steps:

1. First, install a set of supporting libraries by typing `sudo apt-get install libusb-1.0-0-dev mono-runtime libmono-winforms2.0-cil`.

2. Then, copy the configuration file by typing `sudo cp 99-pololu.rules /etc/udev/rules.d/`.

Unfortunately, you can't run `MaestroControlCenter` on your Rasbperry Pi, your version of windowing doesn't support the graphics, but you can control your servos using the `UscCmd` command-line application to ensure that they are connected and working correctly. First, type `./UscCmd --list`, and you should see the following:

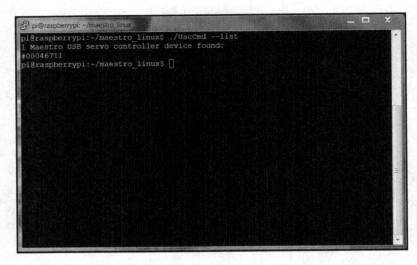

```
pi@raspberrypi:~/maestro_linux$ ./UscCmd --list
1 Maestro USB servo controller device found:
#00046711
pi@raspberrypi:~/maestro_linux$
```

The unit sees your servo controller. If you just type `./UscCmd`, you can see all the commands that you could send to your controller:

```
UscCmd, Version=1.3.0.0, Culture=neutral, PublicKeyToken=null
Select one of the following actions:
  --list                 list available devices
  --configure FILE       load configuration file into device
  --getconf FILE         read device settings and write configuration file
  --restoredefaults      restore factory settings
  --program FILE         compile and load bytecode program
  --status               display complete device status
  --bootloader           put device into bootloader (firmware upgrade) mode
  --stop                 stops the script running on the device
  --start                starts the script running on the device
  --restart              restarts the script at the beginning
  --step                 runs a single instruction of the script
  --sub NUM              calls subroutine n (can be hex or decimal)
  --sub NUM,PARAMETER    calls subroutine n with a parameter (hex or decimal)
                         placed on the stack
  --servo NUM,TARGET     sets the target of servo NUM in units of
                         1/4 microsecond
  --speed NUM,SPEED      sets the speed limit of servo NUM
  --accel NUM,ACCEL      sets the acceleration of servo NUM to a value 0-255
Select which device to perform the action on (optional):
  --device 00001430      (optional) select device #00001430

pi@raspberrypi:~/maestro_linux$
```

Notice how you can send a servo a specific target angle, although the target is not in angle values so it makes it a bit difficult to know where you are sending your servo. Try typing `./UscCmd --servo 0, 10.` The servo will move to its full angle position. Type `./UscCmd - servo 0, 0,` and it will stop the servo from trying to move. In the next section, you'll write some Python code that will translate your angles to the commands that the servo controller will want to see to move it to specific angle locations.

 If you didn't run the Windows version of Maestro Controller and set the **Serial Settings** to **USB Chained,** your motor controller may not respond. Rerun the `MaestroController` code and set the **Serial Settings** to **USB Chained**.

Controlling your hand

You now know that you can talk to your servo motor controller and move your servos. In this section, you'll create a Python program that will let you talk to your servos to move them to specific angles.

Let's start with a simple program that sets the servos to one end of the range (which should open the hand) and then go the other end of the range (which should close your hand). This program starts with the code you wrote in Chapter 3, *Building a Wall-E Robot*. Here is the basic code to control the servos:

```python
#!/usr/bin/python
import serial
import time
def setAngle(ser, channel, angle):
    minAngle = 0.0
    maxAngle = 180.0
    minTarget = 256.0
    maxTarget = 13120.0
    scaledValue = int((angle / ((maxAngle - minAngle) / (maxTarget -
minTarget))) + minTarget)
    commandByte = chr(0x84)
    channelByte = chr(channel)
    lowTargetByte = chr(scaledValue & 0x7F)
    highTargetByte = chr((scaledValue >> 7) & 0x7F)
    command = commandByte + channelByte + lowTargetByte + highTargetByte
    ser.write(command)
    ser.flush()
def setSpeed(ser, channel, speed):
    if speed > 127 or speed <0:
        speed=1
    commandByte = chr(0x87)
```

```
        channelByte = chr(channel)
        highByte, lowByte = divmod(speed,32)
        highTargetByte = chr(highByte)
        lowTargetByte = chr(lowByte << 2)
        command = commandByte + channelByte + lowTargetByte + highTargetByte
        ser.write(command)
        ser.flush()
def setHome(ser):
        for i in range(0, 5):
            setAngle(ser, i ,90)

ser = serial.Serial("/dev/ttyACM0", 9600)
setHome(ser)
time.sleep(1)
```

Here is an explanation of the code:

- `#! /usr/bin/python`: This first line allows you to make this Python file execute from the command line.
- `import serial`: This line imports the serial library. You need the serial library to talk to your unit via USB.
- `def setAngle(ser, channel, angle)`: This function converts your desired setting of servo and angle into the serial command that the servo motor controller needs.
- `def setSpeed(ser, channel, angle)`: This function converts your desired setting of servo and speed into the serial command that the servo motor controller needs.
- `def setHome(ser)`: This function sets each servo to the middle position. This should open your fingers halfway. If your hand isn't in the middle position, you can adjust it by adjusting the position of the servo horns on each servo.
- `ser = serial.Serial("/dev/ttyACM0", 9600)`: This opens the serial port connection to your servo controller.

To access the serial port, you'll need to make sure you have the Python serial library. If you don't, then type `sudo apt-get install python-serial`. After you have installed the serial library you can run your program by typing `sudo python hand.py`.

Now that you have the basic positioning capability, you'll need to create a program that takes command arguments that can position each finger. In this case, we'll keep it simple, assuming that we'll position either open, closed, or halfway in between. Here is the code:

```
#!/usr/bin/python
import serial
```

```
import time
import sys

THUMBOPEN = 110
THUMBCLOSE = 50
INDEXOPEN = 100
INDEXCLOSE = 50
MIDDLEOPEN = 50
MIDDLECLOSE = 110
RINGOPEN = 60
RINGCLOSE = 110
PINKYOPEN = 50
PINKYCLOSE = 110
def setAngle(ser, channel, angle):
    minAngle = 0.0
    maxAngle = 180.0
    minTarget = 256.0
    maxTarget = 13120.0
    scaledValue = int((angle / ((maxAngle - minAngle) / (maxTarget -
minTarget))) + minTarget)
    commandByte = chr(0x84)
    channelByte = chr(channel)
    lowTargetByte = chr(scaledValue & 0x7F)
    highTargetByte = chr((scaledValue >> 7) & 0x7F)
    command = commandByte + channelByte + lowTargetByte + highTargetByte
    ser.write(command)
    ser.flush()
def setSpeed(ser, channel,speed):
    if speed > 127 or speed <0:
        speed=1
    commandByte = chr(0x87)
    channelByte = chr(channel)
    highByte, lowByte = divmod(speed,32)
    highTargetByte = chr(highByte)
    lowTargetByte = chr(lowByte << 2)
    command = commandByte + channelByte + lowTargetByte + highTargetByte
    ser.write(command)
    ser.flush()

def thumb(ser, angle):
    setSpeed(ser, 0, 30)
    setAngle(ser, 0, angle)

def index(ser, angle):
    setSpeed(ser, 1, 30)
    setAngle(ser, 1, angle)

def middle(ser, angle):
```

```
        setSpeed(ser, 2, 30)
        setAngle(ser, 2, angle)

    def ring(ser, angle):
        setSpeed(ser, 3, 30)
        setAngle(ser, 3, angle)

    def pinky(ser, angle):
        setSpeed(ser, 4, 30)
        setAngle(ser, 4, angle)
    ser = serial.Serial("/dev/ttyACM0", 9600)
    if int(sys.argv[1]) == 1:
        if int(sys.argv[2]) == 1:
            angle = THUMBOPEN
        elif int(sys.argv[2]) == 2:
            angle = THUMBCLOSE
        else:
            angle = THUMBOPEN - THUMBCLOSE
        thumb(ser, angle)
    if int(sys.argv[1]) == 2:
        if int(sys.argv[2]) == 1:
            angle = INDEXOPEN
        elif int(sys.argv[2]) == 2:
            angle = INDEXCLOSE
        else:
            angle = INDEXOPEN - INDEXCLOSE
        index(ser, angle)
    if int(sys.argv[1]) == 3:
        if int(sys.argv[2]) == 1:
            angle = MIDDLEOPEN
        elif int(sys.argv[2]) == 2:
            angle = MIDDLECLOSE
        else:
            angle = MIDDLECLOSE - MIDDLEOPEN
        middle(ser, angle)
    if int(sys.argv[1]) == 4:
        if int(sys.argv[2]) == 1:
            angle = RINGOPEN
        elif int(sys.argv[2]) == 2:
            angle = RINGCLOSE
        else:
            angle = RINGCLOSE - RINGOPEN
        ring(ser, angle)
    if int(sys.argv[1]) == 4:
        if int(sys.argv[2]) == 1:
            angle = PINKYOPEN
        elif int(sys.argv[2]) == 2:
            angle = PINKYCLOSE
```

```
else:
    angle = PINKYCLOSE - PINKYOPEN
pinky(ser, angle)
```

Here, each finger can be positioned by calling the program with two arguments, the first is the finger you desire to control, the second is the position, 1 for open, 2 for closed, and 3 (or any other number) for halfway in between.

Here are the specifics for the program additions:

- The constants at the top of the program help you to set the actual angle position for each digit for open and closed.
- The thumb (ser, angle), index (ser, angle), middle (ser, angle), ring (ser, angle), and pinky (ser, angle) allow the program to set that particular finger to a specific angle.
- The `if` statements translate the argument to the correct finger and angle. The first argument specifies the finger, and the second whether you want it closed or open.

You can run this program by typing `./handPosition.py 1.1`, for example, and the thumb should go to the open position. Now that you can position each finger, you'll need a program that can read the position of your hand and then set the hand to the proper position.

Following your hand

It is essential to be able to see if you want to follow your hand. Fortunately, adding hardware and software for vision is both easy and inexpensive. As you learned in Chapter 2, *Building Your Own Futuristic Robot*, connecting a USB camera is very easy.

Most importantly, OpenCV and your webcam can track your hand position. OpenCV makes this amazingly simple by providing some high-level libraries that can help us with this task. First, follow the instructions in Chapter 2, *Building Your Own Futuristic Robot*, to install your USB webcam and OpenCV.

Then you'll create a set of code that looks like this:

```
#!/usr/bin/python
import cv2
import numpy as np
import math
```

```
cap = cv2.VideoCapture(0)
cap.set(3, 360)
cap.set(4, 240)

while(cap.isOpened()):
    ret, img = cap.read()
    grey_image = cv2.cvtColor(img, cv2.COLOR_BGR2GRAY)
    blur = cv2.GaussianBlur(grey_image, (5,5), 0)
    ret, thresh1 = cv2.threshold(blur, 80, 255,
cv2.THRESH_BINARY_INV+cv2.THRESH_OTSU)
    cv2.imshow('Thresholded', thresh1)
    if cv2.waitKey(10) == 27:
        break
cap.release()
cv2.destroyAllWindows()
```

This code makes it possible to isolate your hand. Run the program. Now take your target (in this case, your hand) and move it into the frame. You should see something similar to the following screenshot:

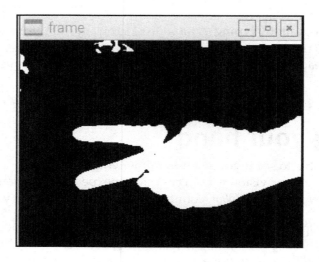

Notice the white pixels in our threshold image showing where your hand is located. You can add more OpenCV code that gives the actual location and size of your hand. In your original image file of your hand, you can actually draw a rectangle around your hand as an indicator. Edit the file as follows:

```python
#!/usr/bin/python
import cv2
import numpy as np
import math

cap = cv2.VideoCapture(0)
cap.set(3, 360)
cap.set(4, 240)

while(cap.isOpened()):
    ret, img = cap.read()
    grey_image = cv2.cvtColor(img, cv2.COLOR_BGR2GRAY)
    blur = cv2.GaussianBlur(grey_image, (5,5), 0)
    ret, thresh1 = cv2.threshold(blur, 80, 255,
cv2.THRESH_BINARY_INV+cv2.THRESH_OTSU)
    contours, hierarchy = cv2.findContours(thresh1.copy(), cv2.RETR_TREE,
cv2.CHAIN_APPROX_NONE)
    max_area = -1
    ci = 0
    for i in range(len(contours)):
        cnt = contours[i]
        area = cv2.contourArea(cnt)
        if (area > max_area):
            max_area = area
            ci = i
    if ci > 0:
        cnt = contours[ci]
        x,y,w,h = cv2.boundingRect(cnt)
        print x, y, w, h
        cv2.rectangle(img, (x, y), (x + w, y + h), (0, 0, 255), 0)
    cv2.imshow('Hand', img)
    cv2.imshow('Thresholded', thresh1)
    if cv2.waitKey(10) == 27:
        break
cap.release()
cv2.destroyAllWindows()
```

Now that the code is ready, you can run it. You should see something similar to the following screenshot:

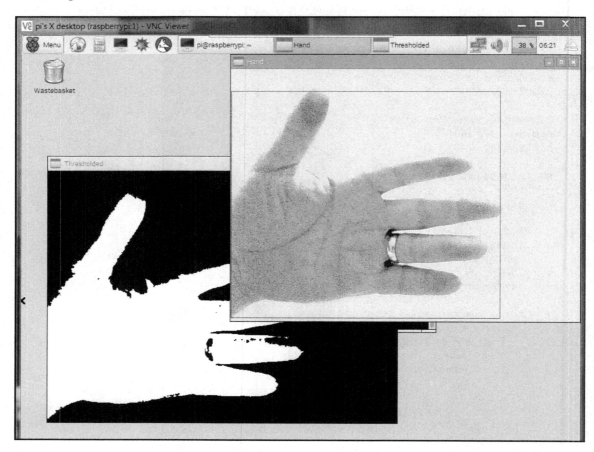

You can now track your hand. You can also see the x, y, length, and width relative measures of your hand. There are a number of ways to determine the actual position of each finger and then move the hand accordingly. There are some quite complex approaches to this, see `http://sa-cybernetics.github.io/blog/213/8/12/hand-tracking-and-recog nition-with-opencv/` and `https://www.javacodegeeks.com/212/12/hand-and-finger-detection-using-javacv.html`.

But let's keep this simple, approximating the position of the hand and then move the fingers accordingly. In this case, you'll assume that the thumb can open and close and the fingers will also open and close together. The rectangle of the shape of your hand can be used for that. If the rectangle is large, then all the fingers are extended. If the rectangle is smaller, then you'll move the fingers to half open. If the rectangle is small, then you can move the fingers to close it fully. Here is the code:

```python
#!/usr/bin/python
import cv2
import numpy as np
import math
import serial
import time

THUMBOPEN = 110
THUMBCLOSE = 50
INDEXOPEN = 100
INDEXCLOSE = 50
MIDDLEOPEN = 50
MIDDLECLOSE = 110
RINGOPEN = 60
RINGCLOSE = 110
PINKYOPEN = 50
PINKYCLOSE = 110

def setAngle(ser, channel, angle):
    minAngle = 0.0
    maxAngle = 180.0
    minTarget = 256.0
    maxTarget = 13120.0
    scaledValue = int((angle / ((maxAngle - minAngle) / (maxTarget -
minTarget))) + minTarget)
    commandByte = chr(0x84)
    channelByte = chr(channel)
    lowTargetByte = chr(scaledValue & 0x7F)
    highTargetByte = chr((scaledValue >> 7) & 0x7F)
    command = commandByte + channelByte + lowTargetByte + highTargetByte
    ser.write(command)
    ser.flush()
```

```
def setSpeed(ser, channel,speed):
    if speed > 127 or speed <0:
        speed=1
    commandByte = chr(0x87)
    channelByte = chr(channel)
    highByte, lowByte = divmod(speed,32)
    highTargetByte = chr(highByte)
    lowTargetByte = chr(lowByte << 2)
    command = commandByte + channelByte + lowTargetByte + highTargetByte
    ser.write(command)
    ser.flush()

cap = cv2.VideoCapture(0)
cap.set(3, 720)
cap.set(4, 480)
ser = serial.Serial("/dev/ttyACM0", 9600)
while(cap.isOpened()):
    ret, img = cap.read()
    grey_image = cv2.cvtColor(img, cv2.COLOR_BGR2GRAY)
    blur = cv2.GaussianBlur(grey_image, (5,5), 0)
    ret, thresh1 = cv2.threshold(blur, 80, 255,
cv2.THRESH_BINARY_INV+cv2.THRESH_OTSU)
    contours, hierarchy = cv2.findContours(thresh1.copy(), cv2.RETR_TREE,
cv2.CHAIN_APPROX_NONE)
    max_area = -1
    ci = 0
    for i in range(len(contours)):
        cnt = contours[i]
        area = cv2.contourArea(cnt)
        if (area > max_area):
            max_area = area
            ci = i
    if ci > 0:
        cnt = contours[ci]
        x,y,w,h = cv2.boundingRect(cnt)
        cv2.rectangle(img, (x, y), (x + w, y + h), (0, 0, 255), 0)
        if h < 300:
            setSpeed(ser, 0, 30)
            setAngle(ser, 0, THUMBCLOSE)
        else:
            setSpeed(ser, 0, 30)
            setAngle(ser, 0, THUMBOPEN)
        if w < 300:
            setSpeed(ser, 1, 30)
            setAngle(ser, 1, INDEXCLOSE)
            setSpeed(ser, 2, 30)
            setAngle(ser, 2, MIDDLECLOSE)
            setSpeed(ser, 3, 30)
```

```
            setAngle(ser, 3, RINGCLOSE)
            setSpeed(ser, 4, 30)
            setAngle(ser, 4, PINKYCLOSE)
        else:
            setSpeed(ser, 1, 30)
            setAngle(ser, 1, INDEXOPEN)
            setSpeed(ser, 2, 30)
            setAngle(ser, 2, MIDDLEOPEN)
            setSpeed(ser, 3, 30)
            setAngle(ser, 3, RINGOPEN)
            setSpeed(ser, 4, 30)
            setAngle(ser, 4, PINKYOPEN)
    cv2.imshow('Hand', img)
    if cv2.waitKey(10) == 27:
        break
cap.release()
cv2.destroyAllWindows()
```

Once you have the code entered, you can run the program. When you open your hand completely the hand should open completely, and you should see this on the screen:

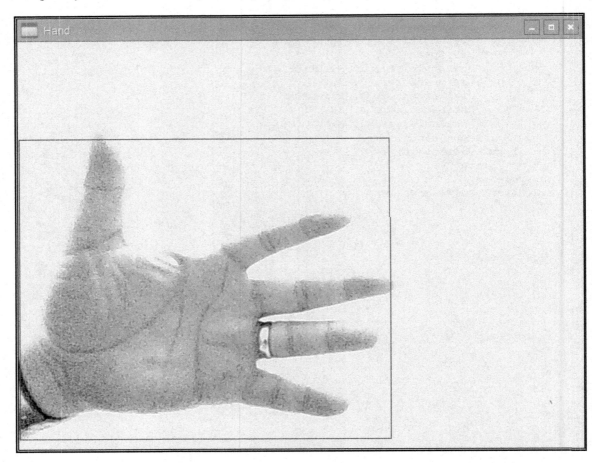

When you close your hand, the robotic hand should close and you should see this on the screen:

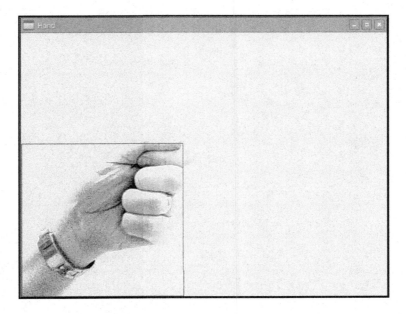

You may need to position your hand or change *w* and *h* compare values, in this code set to 300, in the program so it can sense a large rectangle when your hand is open, and a small rectangle when your hand is closed. You can also now review the more complex finger sensing algorithms so that you can sense the position of each individual finger and then send the appropriate `setAngle` command.

Summary

You now have a hand that can move as your hand moves! By now you should have quite a few different capabilities that you can add to almost any project. In the next chapter, you'll add Raspberry Pi to a self-balancing, two-wheeled robot.

6
A Self-Balancing Robot

Now that you've built an astounding number of cool projects, you are ready to take on a slightly more complex technical challenge; building a robot that can balance on two wheels. This type of vehicle was unknown until the advent of the Segway and now has seen lots of new interest with hover boards that allow users mobility in a very small size.

In this chapter, you'll learn the following:

- How to build a self-balancing, two-wheeled robot
- How to use control theory to make your robot stable

Let's get started by building a simple hardware platform.

Creating the hardware platform

As you might suspect, your hardware platform will begin with two DC motors and two wheels. You'll also need a simple hardware set to which you can attach your motors and wheels. You can either purchase pieces, or an entire kit, such as the one offered at http://www.sainsmart.com/sainsmart-balancing-robot-kit.html.

If you are buying pieces you'll want to start with two DC motors with encoders, such as the 9.7:1 Metal Gearmotor 25Dx48L mm LP 6V with 48 CPR Encoder available at htttp://www.pololu.com or http://www.amazon.com. You'll also want wheels that fit these motors, both http://www.pololu.com and http://www.amazon.com have these as well.

You'll need some acrylic parts that allow you to attach the wheels as well as the battery and Raspberry Pi. Here is an image of the kit parts assembled with the motors and wheels. You can certainly cut your own parts from acrylic. Either way, here is the completed basic platform:

Now you'll need to add the electronics.

Adding the electronics to your platform

The basic hardware platform is ready, and adding the Raspberry Pi is quite simple. You'll use the same RaspiRobot board that you used in Chapter 2, *Building Your Own Futuristic Robot*. Here is an image of the board mounted on the Raspberry Pi:

You'll need to connect the RaspiRobot to the DC motors. This is quite simple; you'll only use two of the six connectors on the motors. The rest are to power and read the encoders; you'll not use these on this project. Here is an image of the motor connector:

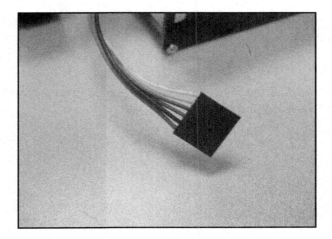

You'll need to connect the **black** connector to one of the **L** connectors on the RaspiRobot board, and the **red** connector to the **L** connector on the RaspiRobot board. Connect the second motor to the **R** connectors. Then connect a battery to the **GND** and **+V** connectors; you'll want to use a 3S LiPo battery that can supply 11.1 V. The next step is to start controlling the DC motors.

Controlling the DC motors

To control the DC motors from the Raspberry Pi, you'll first want to install the libraries. Here are the steps to do so:

1. `cd ~`: Go to the home directory.
2. `git clone https://github.com/simonmonk/raspirobotboard3.git`: This command will get the library.
3. `cd raspirobotboard3/python`: Go to the directory that has the installed files.
4. `sudo python setup.py install`: Install the Python library.

Once these are installed, you can write this simple program to make the wheels go forward:

```
#!/usr/bin/python
from rrb3 import *
import time
rr = RRB3(11, 11)
rr.set_motors(0.5, 0, 0.5, 0)
time.sleep(1)
rr.set_motors(0, 0, 0, 0)
```

This should make the wheels go forward at half the speed. You can add a bit of code to check full speed and forward and backward:

```
#!/usr/bin/python
from rrb3 import *
import time
rr = RRB3(11, 11)
rr.set_motors(1, 0, 1, 0)
time.sleep(1)
rr.set_motors(0.5, 0, 0.5, 0)
time.sleep(1)
rr.set_motors(0.5, 1, 0.5, 1)
time.sleep(1)
rr.set_motors(0, 0, 0, 0)
```

Now that you have control over the speed and direction of the wheels, you'll want to connect the **Inertial Measurement Unit (IMU)**

Reading the IMU

The IMU is a special measurement unit that will tell you about the movement of your robot. It uses a combination of accelerometers and gyroscopes, sometimes also magnetometers. This will allow your robot to sense when it is falling over, and then can respond and right itself.

Here is an image of a unit that is available at most online electronic retailers:

The connections to this chip are straightforward, and the device communicates with Raspberry Pi using the I2C bus. Since you are using the motor controller, you can connect the device to the I2C bus on the controller board. Here is a close-up of the I2C connector on the RaspiRobot board:

There are five connections. You'll connect your device **VCC** to the **5V** connection on the motor controller. You'll connect **GND** on your device to **GND** on the motor controller. Then connect the **SCL** connector on your device to the **C** connector on the motor controller and the **SDA** pin on the device to the *D* connection on the motor controller. Notice that you will not connect the other connections. Here is an image of the connections:

Now you are ready to communicate with the device.

Accessing the compass programmatically

In order to access the compass capability you'll need to enable the I2C library on the Raspberry Pi. The first step to enable the IMU is to enable the I2C interface. The I2C interface is a synchronous serial interface, and provides more performance than an asynchronous *Rx/Tx* serial interface. The **SCL** data line provides a clock, while the data flows on the **SDA** line. The bus also provides addressing so that more than one device can be connected to the master device at the same time.

Enabling this bus is done by running `sudo raspi-config`, and selecting the **Advanced Options**, like this:

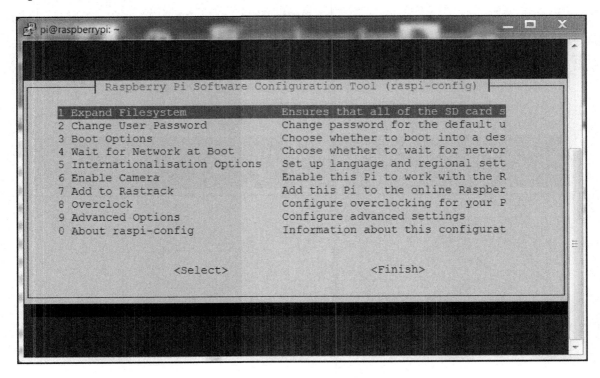

Once there, go to the I2C selection and enable the I2C, like this:

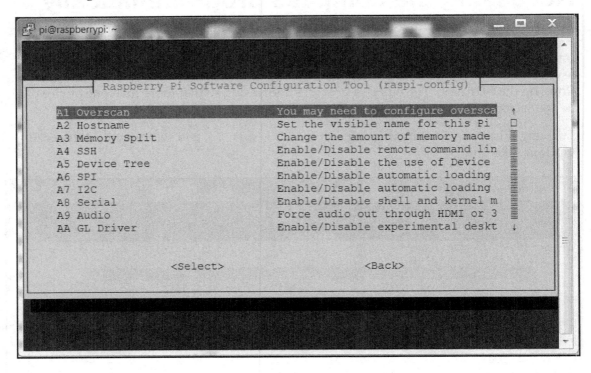

Say yes to all the selections to enable the I2C interface and load the library, then reboot the Raspberry Pi. Install the I2C tool kit by typing `sudo apt-get install i2c-tools`. You can see if the I2C is enabled by typing `sudo i2cdetect -y 1`, and you should see something like this:

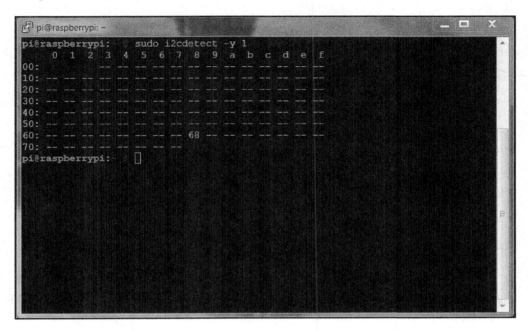

You can see the device at **68**. Now you communicate with your IMU. You'll need to create a Python program to get the data. But before you create your Python code, you'll need to install `smbus` capability to access I2C. You can do this by typing `sudo apt-get install python-smbus`.

There are several good libraries to get the data from the device, but there is some code based on the library at `https://gist.github.com/skfwMelonpan/9fecdb3e91ceae174e`:

```
#!/usr/bin/python
import sys
import smbus
import math
import time
import datetime

powerMgmt1 = 0x6b
# This reads a data byte from the I2C device
def read_byte(adr):
```

```
        return bus.read_byte_data(address, adr)
# This reads a data word from the I2C device
def read_word(adr):
    high = bus.read_byte_data(address, adr)
    low = bus.read_byte_data(address, adr+1)
    val = (high << 8) + low
    return val
# This reads the second data word from the I2C device
def read_word_2c(adr):
    val = read_word(adr)
    if (val >= 0x8000):
        return -((65535 - val) + 1)
    else:
        return val
# This function calculates the distribution of a set of values
def dist(a,b):
    return math.sqrt((a*a)+(b*b))
# This function calculates the y rotation for the x, y, and z values
def get_y_rotation(x,y,z):
    radians = math.atan2(x, dist(y,z))
    return -math.degrees(radians)
# This function calculates the x rotation for the x, y, and z values
def get_x_rotation(x,y,z):
    radians = math.atan2(y, dist(x,z))
    return math.degrees(radians)
# Create a smbbus instance
bus = smbus.SMBus(1)
# Set this to the address of the I2C device
address = 0x68
# Setup for the IMC
bus.write_byte_data(address, powerMgmt1, 0)
# Get the current time and set the start variable
start = datetime.datetime.now()
# Get the current delta time and set the end variable.
end = start+datetime.timedelta(seconds=60)
# Get the current time and set the now variable.
now = datetime.datetime.now()
# Do this loop forever.
while 1:
    # Get the gyro and acceleration values from the IMC device.
    gyroXout = read_word_2c(0x43)
    gyroYout = read_word_2c(0x45)
    gyroZout = read_word_2c(0x47)

    accelXout = read_word_2c(0x3b)
    accelYout = read_word_2c(0x3d)
    accelZout = read_word_2c(0x3f)
# Print out the gyro and acceleration values from the IMC device.
```

```
print datetime.datetime.now()-start
print accelXout
print accelYout
print accelZout
print gyroXout
print gyroYout
print gyroZout
time.sleep(.5)
if end-datetime.datetime.now()<datetime.timedelta(seconds=0):
    sys.exit(0)
```

If you run this code you will see the acceleration and position data being printed out. Now that you have access to this data you can start working on the balancing algorithm.

The balancing algorithm

Building a balancing robot provides some interesting control channels. Fortunately, there are several good tutorials for this sort of thing, for example, at `http://ozzmaker.com/succ ess-with-a-balancing-robot-using-a-raspberry-pi/`.

To understand the problem, let's look at your robot. Here is an image of the assembled robot from the side:

What you'll be doing now is using the output of the IMU to determine that angle of the robot. If the robot is leaning too far forward, you'll move the wheels quickly forward to push the robot back upward. The same is true if the robot is leaning too far backward.

To make this all work, you'll need to implement a **Proportional-Integration-Derivative (PID)** controller. A brief tutorial is probably in order. Here is a block diagram of a control loop:

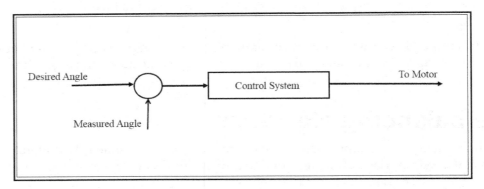

The **Desired Angle** is the angle of the IMU when the robot is straight up and down. The **Measured Angle** is the angle that is actually measured from the IMU. If the angle is too far forward or too far backward then the **Control System** will move the motors to correct the error in position. This is called a feedback loop. The motor sets the angle, so you are feeding the current angle back into the system.

To be most efficient, the **Control System** will contain three separate elements: **Proportional, Derivative**, and **Integral**. Here is a block diagram of the elements:

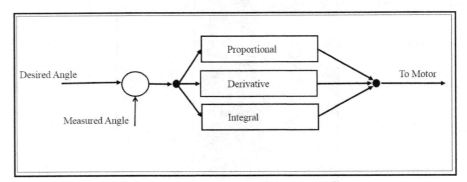

The **Proportional (P)** element of the PID controller is directly based on the current angle difference from the **Desired Angle** (where the robot balances). This difference will be multiplied by the P gain. The P gain is the gain you'll need to adjust to get the right amount of **Proportional** control. The **Integral (I)** element of the PID controller is based on the current angle difference or error from the desired angle (where the robot balances) accumulated over time. The **Integral** control assists in balancing the robot if it is moving. The **Derivative (D)** element of the PID controller is based on the current rate of change of the angle difference between the current angle and the desired angle (where the robot balances). It is used to dampen the response as the robot reaches **Zero Point**. Without the **Derivative** control, the position of the robot can overshoot and start to oscillate.

The sum of all three of these is used to control the motor. In the PID controller code, you'll be able to adjust how much of each of these elements will be used in the final code by adjusting the gain for each element. There are several good examples of Python PID library code available. A simple but useful version is available at http://code.activestate.com/recipes/577231-discrete-pid-controller/.

The most important function, from your perspective, will be the update function of the controller. Here, the PID controller will use the current_value of the angle, compare it with the set_point, and then use all three elements of the PID controller to create the desired control signal to the motor, in this case, a speed that you will send to your motors. There is also an initialization function, as well as a way to set the gains for all three different elements.

You'll need this code in the directory for your main robot control, and you'll include it as a library. You'll need two additional libraries for your program. The first is some code to access the capabilities of the 6050 IMU. Again, there are several excellent libraries that are available to do this; here is the link for the code for one of them: https://github.com/bitify/raspi/blob/master/i2c-sensors/bitify/python/sensors/mpu65.py.

The final library you'll need is a library to control the motors. You'll need to create that Python file and save it as motor.py. Here is the code:

```python
#!/usr/bin/python
from rrb3 import *
import time
rr = RRB3(11, 11)

def motor_forward(speed):
    if speed > 1:
        speed = 1
    if speed < 0:
        speed = 0
    rr.set_motors(speed, 0, speed, 0)
```

```
def motor_reverse(speed):
    if speed > 1:
        speed = 1
    if speed < 0:
        speed = 0
    rr.set_motors(speed, 1, speed, 1)

def motor_stop():
    rr.set_motors(0, 0, 0, 0)
```

Now you'll need some code to bring all this capability together, so you'll want to create a Python code that will contain the main control loop. Make sure the libraries described earlier are in the same directory as the directory of this file. You'll want to make sure that there is an `mpu6050.py`, a `PID.py`, and a `motor.py` file in the directory.

In this main control loop code, you'll include the libraries and then, in a `while` loop, measure the current angle, call the PID library to calculate the new `speed` value to send to the motors, and then send it to the motors. Here is that code:

```
#!/usr/bin/python
import smbus
import math
import time
from mpu6050 import MPU6050
from PID import PID
from motor import *
gyro_scale = 131.0
accel_scale = 16384.0
RAD_TO_DEG = 57.29578
M_PI = 3.14159265358979323846
address = 0x68
bus = smbus.SMBus(1)
now = time.time()
K = 0.98
K1 = 1 - K
time_diff = 0.01
sensor = MPU6050(bus, address, "MPU6050")
sensor.read_raw_data()
rate_gyroX = 0.0
rate_gyroY = 0.0
rate_gyroZ = 0.0
gyroAngleX = 0.0
gyroAngleY = 0.0
gyroAngleZ = 0.0
raw_accX = 0.0
raw_accY = 0.0
raw_accZ = 0.0
```

```
rate_accX = 0.0
rate_accY = 0.0
rate_accZ = 0.0
accAngX1 = 0.0
CFangleX1 = 0.0
FIX = -12.89
def dist(a, b):
    return math.sqrt((a * a) + (b * b))

def get_y_rotation(x,y,z):
    radians = math.atan2(x, dist(y,z))
    return -math.degrees(radians)

def get_x_rotation(x,y,z):
    radians = math.atan2(y, dist(x,z))
    return math.degrees(radians)

p=PID(1.0,-0.04,0.0)
p.setPoint(0.0)
for i in range(0, int(300.0 / time_diff)):
    time.sleep(time_diff - 0.005)
    sensor.read_raw_data()
    rate_gyroX = sensor.read_scaled_gyro_x()
    rate_gyroY = sensor.read_scaled_gyro_y()
    rate_gyroZ = sensor.read_scaled_gyro_z()
    gyroAngleX += rate_gyroX * time_diff
    gyroAngleY += rate_gyroY * time_diff
    gyroAngleZ += rate_gyroZ * time_diff
    raw_accX = sensor.read_raw_accel_x()
    raw_accY = sensor.read_raw_accel_y()
    raw_accZ = sensor.read_raw_accel_z()
    rate_accX = sensor.read_scaled_accel_x()
    rate_accY = sensor.read_scaled_accel_y()
    rate_accZ = sensor.read_scaled_accel_z()
    accAngX1 = get_x_rotation(rate_accX, rate_accY, rate_accX)
    CFangleX1 = ( K * ( CFangleX1 + rate_gyroX * time_diff) + (1 - K) *
accAngX1 )

    pid = (p.update(CFangleX1))
    speed = pid/10.0
    print CFangleX1
    print speed

    if(pid > 0):
        motor_forward(speed)
    elif(pid < 0):
        motor_reverse( abs(speed) )
    else:
```

```
motor_stop()
```

There is quite a bit of code here, but most of it is to set up the system. However, one of the key lines of code is the line with `p=PID(1.0,-0.04,0.0)`. This initializes the PID controller with the value for the gain for the Proportional control, the gain for the Derivative control, and finally the gain for the Integral control. As is often the case, the Integral control can be set at 0. The values for the Proportional and Derivative control will need to be adjusted for each robot to make sure it is stable and controls the robot to keep it upright. In order to do this for your robot, you'll need to adjust these gains. Here are the steps to setting these two values:

1. Set the gain of the Integrative control and the gain of the Derivative control to zero.
2. Set the Proportional gain high enough so that the motors drive the wheels under the robot in the direction it is falling. The robot should overshoot the desired angle a bit and then start to oscillate.
3. Reduce the Proportional gain control by about 10%, or until the robot is just below oscillation.
4. Increase the Integrative gain. This will help the robot reach the desired angle faster and will also start the robot oscillating. Try and get a value so that the robot just oscillates.
5. Increase the Derivative gain to dampen the oscillation and until the robot balances.

This is all a very delicate balance, as changing any of the characteristics of the robot will change these values. But once you have them you should have a balancing robot.

Summary

You've built many different amazing robots. Your next robot will take you into the air, literally. You'll add the Raspberry Pi to a quadcopter and build your very own autonomous flying machine.

7
Adding the Raspberry Pi to a Quadcopter

If you've chosen to construct even a few of the projects in this book, you have an amazing array of projects to play with. However, there is one area that you haven't explored yet: flight. This project will help you dive into the area of flight; you'll add the Raspberry Pi to a flying machine to explore the skies.

In this chapter, you'll learn how to do the following:

- Interface the Raspberry Pi with the flight controller on a quadcopter
- Create a system that enables long-range communications
- Add GPS so that you can know where your quadcopter is in order to know your location
- Fly your quadcopter autonomously

Let's get started by adding the Raspberry Pi to a quadcopter platform.

Accessing the hardware platform

There are many ways to approach the enabling of your quadcopter platform. One way is to build it from scratch. However, in this case, you're going to use a well-known, affordable platform to make this task much simpler. You'll use the Parrot 2.0 quadcopter platform, available from many different online retailers. Here is an image of it:

One of the key advantages of using Parrot 2.0 is that it uses a standard WLAN access point as a control interface; your Raspberry Pi can easily access this to gain control. That's it! You've got your hardware platform.

Connecting to the hardware

Connecting to Parrot 2.0 is also quite easy; you'll just need to connect to its WLAN access point. However, to add control via a programming language, such as Python, you'll need to install some libraries for the Raspberry Pi. First, let's download the libraries. You'll get these from `https://github.com/venthur/python-ardrone`. Download the files to your Raspberry Pi by typing wget `https://github.com/venthur/python-ardrone`. Now create a simple program to demonstrate that the system works. Here is the code:

```
import libardrone
from time import sleep
drone = libardrone.ARDrone()
drone.takeoff()
sleep(3)
```

```
drone.move_forward()
sleep(2)
drone.land()
sleep(3)
drone.halt()
```

This program is quite simple. You import the library and create an instance of your quadcopter as a drone. Then you issue a command to have your quadcopter take off and hover for three seconds, after which you move forward for two seconds, then land, and then after three seconds, turn the drone off.

Before you run the program, however, you'll need to connect to the quadcopter. To do this, select the network icon in the upper right-hand corner; it will look like two computers one behind the other. You'll see a menu, as illustrated here:

Now click on the ardrone menu item, and you will see the wireless connections indicator in the upper right-hand corner, like this:

You won't need a password. Once your Raspberry Pi is connected, you can run the simple demo program. Your quadcopter should take off, move forward, and then land. You'll need to mount your Raspberry Pi on the quadcopter and then control your Raspberry Pi remotely. You can do this by using a small wireless keyboard display mounted on the Raspberry Pi and writing a simple program to control the quadcopter using the keys, like this:

```
import libardrone
from time import sleep
import sys
import tty
import termios
# This function gets a single character from the keyboard
def getch():
    fd = sys.stdin.fileno()
    old_settings = termios.tcgetattr(fd)
    tty.setraw(sys.stdin.fileno())
    ch = sys.stdin.read(1)
    termios.tcsetattr(fd, termios.TCSADRAIN, old_settings)
```

```
    return ch
# create an instance of your drone
drone = libardrone.ARDrone()
var = 'n'
print "starting up"
# loop until you encounter a 'q' character, execute the command
while var != 'q':
    var = getch()
    if var == 't':
        drone.takeoff()
    if var == 'f':
        drone.move_forward()
    if var == 'b':
        drone.move_backward()
    if var == 'u':
        drone.move_up()
    if var == 'd':
        drone.move_down()
    if var == 'l':
        drone.move_left()
    if var == 'r':
        drone.move_right()
    if var == 's':
        drone.land()
drone.halt()
```

Now you can control your quadcopter using the Raspberry Pi mounted on the quadcopter!

Remote communication

While you can certainly connect a wireless keyboard to your Raspberry Pi to fly it, you may want to be able to control it from longer than 30 meters or so, which traditional 2.4 GHz wireless keyboards or Bluetooth or WLAN provides. Fortunately, there are devices specially made to connect to Linux systems, such as Raspberry Pi that can provide up to one mile of operating distance along with an RF link.

Make sure you purchase an XBee Series 1 device as it is the easiest device to configure and use, and there is a great open source community support for the device too. If you choose a different device, you'll need to follow the directions for that device provided by the manufacturer. Also, if you want to use this type of point-to-point communication, you'll need two units: one for the Raspberry Pi and the other for the host computer.

The ZigBee standard is built upon the IEEE 802.15.4 standard: a standard that was created to allow a set of devices to communicate with each other in order to enable low data rate coordination of multiple devices. The ZigBee part of the standard ensures interoperability between the vendors of these low-rate devices. The IEEE 802.15.4 part of the standard specifies the physical interface, and the ZigBee part of the standard defines the network and application interface. To find out more about ZigBee, refer to http://www.zigbee.org. Since we are only interested in the physical interface working together, you can buy IEEE 802.15.4 devices. But, ZigBee devices are a bit more prevalent because they are the supersets of IEEE 802.15.4 and are also quite inexpensive.

The other standard that you might hear as you try to purchase or use devices like these is XBee. This is a specific company's implementation, Digi, of several different wireless standards with standard hardware modules that can connect to different embedded systems in many different ways. They make some devices that support ZigBee; the following is an image of this type of device, which supports ZigBee attached to a shield that provides a USB port:

The advantage of using this device is that it is configured to make it very easy to create and manage a simple link between two XBee Series 1 devices. Make sure you have an XBee device that supports ZigBee Series 1. You'll also need to purchase a shield that provides a USB port connection to the device.

Configuring the XBee device

Now, let's get started with configuring your two devices in order to make them talk. I'll give an example here using Windows and a PC. A Linux user can do something similar by using a Linux Terminal program. An excellent tutorial is available at `http://web.univ-pau.fr/~cpham/WSN/XBee.html`.

If you are using Windows, plug one of the devices into your personal computer. Your computer should find the latest drivers for the device. You should see your device when you click on the **Devices and Printers** option from the **Start** menu, as follows:

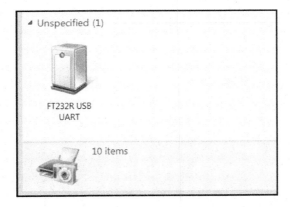

The device is now available to communicate with through the IEEE 802.15.4 wireless interface. We could set up a full ZigBee-compliant network, but because we're just going to communicate from one device to another directly, we'll just use the device as a serial port connection. Double-click on the device icon and then select the **Hardware** tab; you should see the following screenshot:

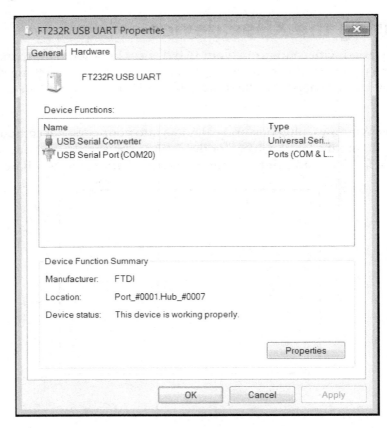

Note that the device is connected to the COM20 serial port. We'll use this to communicate with the device and configure it. You can use any Terminal emulator program; I like to use PuTTY, which is already on my computer. To get PuTTY, go to `http://www.chiark.green` `end.org.uk/~sgtatham/putty/download.html`.

Perform the following steps to configure the device:

1. Open PuTTY and select the **Serial** option and (in this case) the **COM20** port. The following screenshot shows how to fill in the PuTTY window to configure the device:

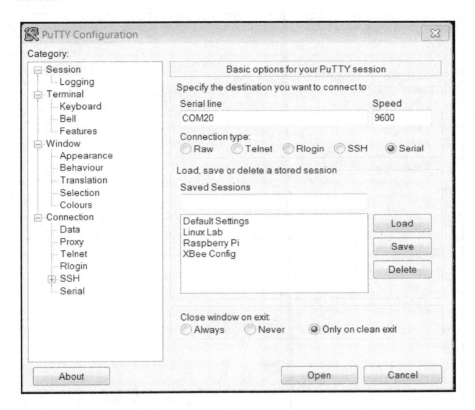

2. Configure the following parameters in the Terminal window (the **Serial** option in the **Category:** selection set): Baud rate as 9600, the **Data bits** option as 8; **Parity** as **None**, and the **Stop bits** option as 1. This is illustrated in the following screenshot:

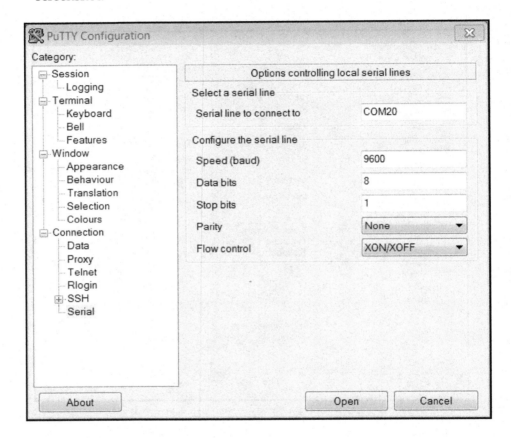

3. Make sure you also select **Force on** for the **Local echo** option and check the **Implicit CR in every LF** and **Implicit LF in every CR** options available under the **Terminal** tab of the **Category:** selection set, as follows:

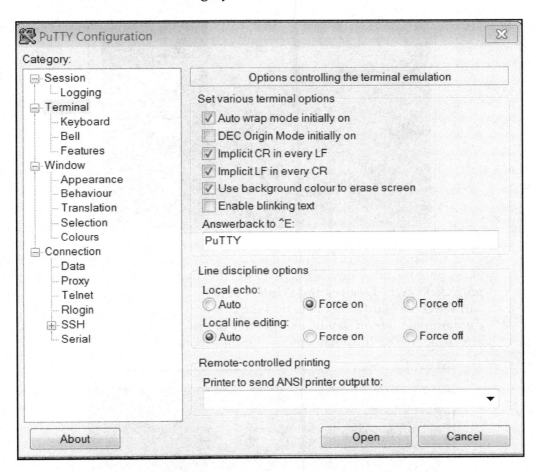

4. Connect to the device by clicking on **Open**.
5. Enter the commands for the device through the Terminal window, as shown in the following screenshot:

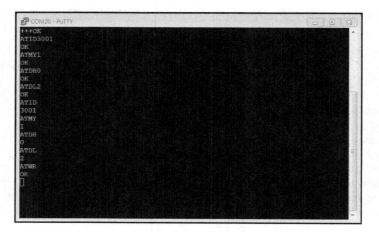

6. The OK response comes from the device as you enter each of these commands. Now, plug the other device into the PC. Note that it might choose a different COM port; click on the **Devices and Printers** option, double-click on the device's icon, and select the **Hardware** tab to find the COM port. Follow the same steps to configure the second device, except there are two changes. The following is a screenshot of the Terminal window for these commands:

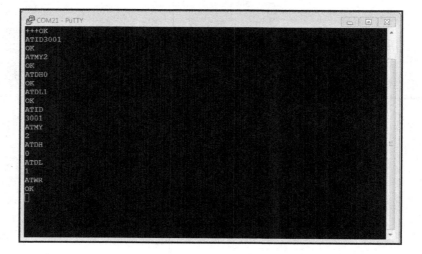

The devices are now ready to talk to one another.

Communicating over the XBee interface

Plug one of the devices into the Raspberry Pi USB port. Using a Terminal window, show the devices that are connected by typing `ls /dev/tty*`. It will look something similar to what is shown in the following screenshot:

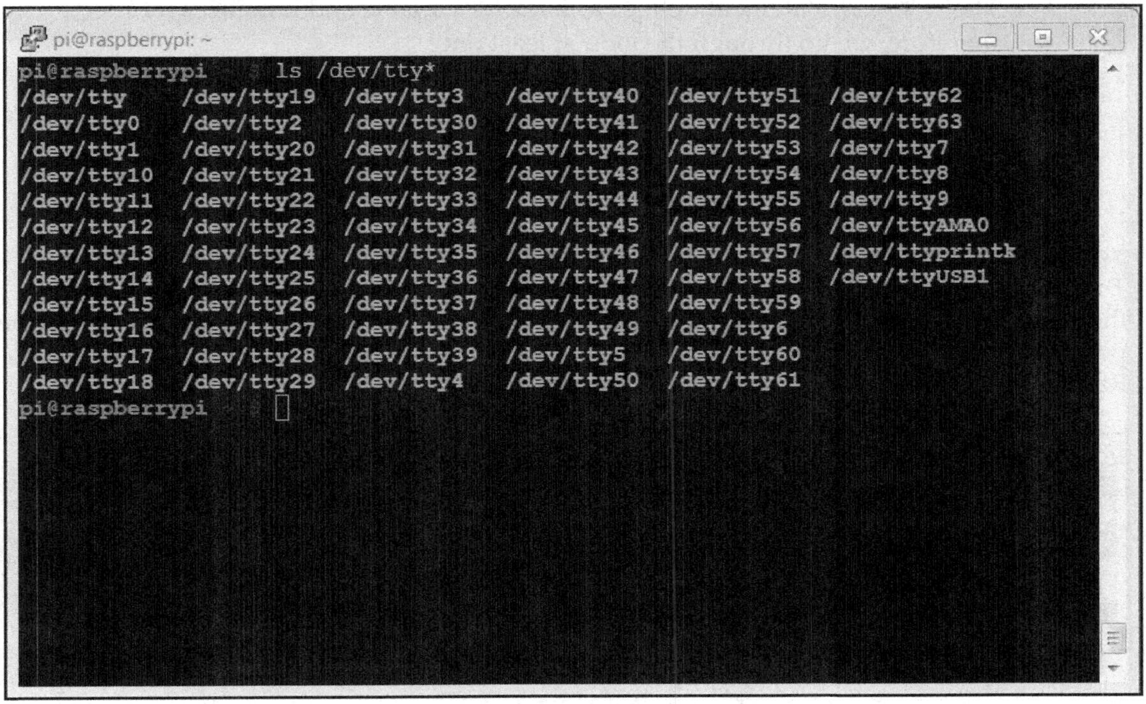

Note that the device appears at `/dev/ttyUSB1`. Now you'll need to create a Python program that will read the preceding input. The following is a listing of such a program:

```
import serial
ser = serial.Serial('/dev/ttyUSB1', 9600, timeout = 1)
x = 'n'
while x!= 'q':
    x = ser.read(1)
    print x
```

The following points explain the functionality of the code:

- The `#!/usr/bin/python` statement allows your program to run without invoking Python on the command line
- The `import serial` statement imports the `Serial` port library
- The `ser = serial.Serial('/dev/ttyUSB1', 9600, timeout = 1)` statement opens a serial port pointing to the `/dev/ttyUSB1` port with a baud rate of `9600` and a timeout of `1`
- The `x = 'n'` statement defines a character variable and initializes it to `'n'`; therefore, we go through the loop at least once
- You will enter the `while` loop, `while x != 'q':`, until the user enters the `q` character
- The `x = ser.read(1)` statement reads 1 byte from the serial port
- The `print x` statement prints out the value

You can now save the program. Consider that you have run `python readData.py` in a Terminal window and have the PuTTY program on your personal computer connected to the other XBee module. If you do this, you should see the characters, which you type on the personal computer's Terminal windows, come out on the Terminal windows running on Raspberry Pi. The following screenshot, with two halves, illustrates these two instances:

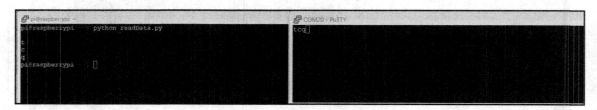

Connecting this functionality to your robot is very easy. Start with the `remote.py` program that you created earlier in the chapter. Copy this to a new program by typing `cp remote.py xbee.py`. Now, let's remove some of the code, parts that you don't need, and add a bit that will accept the character input from the XBee module.

There are only two meaningful changes that happen in the code, as follows:

- `serInput = serial.Serial('/dev/ttyUSB0', 9600, timeout = 1)`: This statement sets up a serial port, getting an input from the XBee device. It is important to note that the `USB0` and `USB1` settings might be different in your specific configuration, based on whether the XBee serial device or the motor controller serial device is configured first.

- `var = serInput.read(1)`: For this statement, instead of getting the input from the user via the keyboard, you will be required to read the characters from the XBee device.

That's it! Now your robot should respond to the commands sent from your Terminal window on your personal computer. You could also create an application on your personal computer that could turn mouse movements or other inputs into proper commands for your robot.

Adding GPS to your quadcopter

To complete the tasks in this chapter, you'll need a USB GPS device, one that connects through an interface supported by the GPIO of the Raspberry Pi. The following image is an example of a device that uses the USB interface:

The model number of the device in the preceding image is ND-100S from GlobalSat. It is small, inexpensive, and supports Windows, Mac OS X, and Linux, so your system should be able to interface with it. It is available on Amazon and other online electronics stores, so you should be able to get it almost anywhere. Now that you have your device, let's look at how to connect it to the Raspberry Pi so that you can start taking data.

Connecting the Raspberry Pi to a USB GPS device

Before you get started, let me give you a brief tutorial on GPS. **GPS**, which stands for **Global Positioning System**, is a system of satellites that transmit signals. GPS devices use these signals to calculate the position of an object. There are a total of 24 satellites transmitting signals all around the Earth at any given moment, but your device can only *see* the signal from a much smaller set of satellites.

Each of these satellites transmits a very accurate time signal that your device can receive and interpret. It receives the time signal from each of these satellites, and then based on the delay—the time it takes the signal to reach the device—it calculates the receiver's position, which is in turn based on a procedure called triangulation. The next two diagrams illustrate how a device uses the difference between the delay data from three satellites to calculate its position. The following is the first diagram, depicting the device at its initial position:

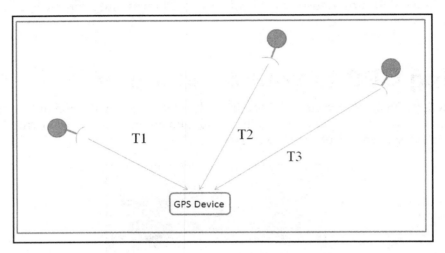

The GPS device is able to detect the three signals and the time delays associated with receiving them. In the following diagram, the device is at a different location, and the time delays associated with the three signals have changed from those in the previous diagram:

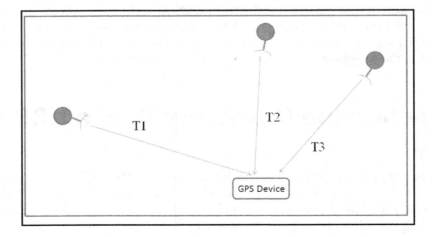

The time delays of the signals **T1**, **T2**, and **T3** can provide the GPS with an absolute position using triangulation. Since the positions of the satellites are known, the amount of time that the signal takes to reach the GPS device is also a measure of the distance between that satellite and the GPS device. To simplify this concept, let's see an example in two dimensions. If the GPS device knows its distance from one satellite, based on the amount of time delay, you could draw a circle around the satellite at that distance and know that your GPS device is on the boundary of that sphere, as shown in the following diagram:

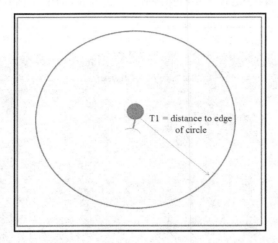

If you have two satellites' signals and know the distance between them, you can draw two circles, as shown in the following diagram:

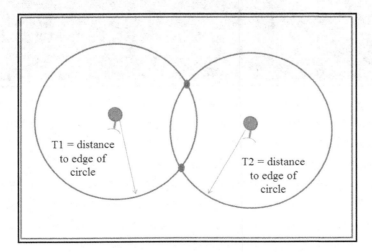

However, you know that since you can only be at the points on the boundary of the circle, you must be at one of the two points that are on the boundary of both the circles. Adding an additional satellite would eliminate one of these two points, providing your exact location. You need more satellites if you are going to do this in all three dimensions.

Now it's time to connect the device. First, connect the GPS unit by plugging it into one of the free USB ports on the USB hub. Once it is plugged in and the unit is rebooted, type lsusb and you should see the output shown in the following screenshot:

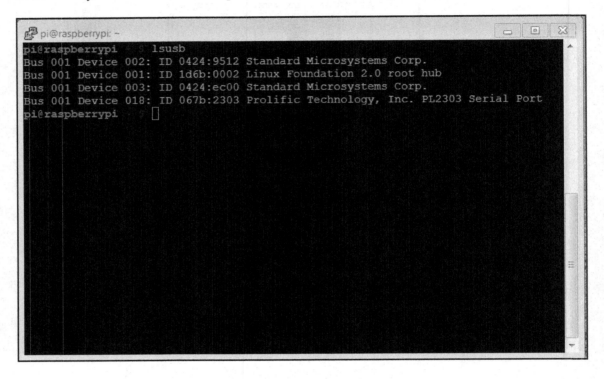

The device is shown as **Prolific Technology, Inc. PL2303 Serial Port**. Your device is now connected to your Raspberry Pi. Now create a simple Python program that will read the value from the GPS device. If you are using the Emacs editor, type emacs measgps.py. A new file will be created called measgps.py. Then type the following:

```
#!/usr/bin/python
import serial
ser = serial.Serial('/dev/ttypUSB0', 4800, timeout = 1)
x = ser.read(1200)
print x
```

Let's go through the code to see what is happening:

- #!/usr/bin/python: As discussed earlier, this line simply makes this file available for you to execute from the command line.

- import serial: This imports the serial library. This will allow you to interface the USB GPS sensor with the GPS system.

- ser = serial.Serial('/dev/ttyUSB0', 4800, timeout = 1): This command sets up the serial port to use the /dev/ttyUSB0 device, which is your GPS sensor using a baud rate of 4800 and a timeout value of 1 second.

- x = ser.read(1200): This command then reads a set of values from the USB port. In this case, you read 1200 bytes; this includes a fairly complete set of your GPS data.

- print x: This command then prints out the value obtained from the previous command.

Once you have created this file, you can run the program and talk to the device. Do this by typing python measgps.py, and the program will run. You should see the output shown in the following screenshot:

```
pi@raspberrypi: ~

$GPGSA,A,1,,,,,,,,,,,,,,,*1E
$GPRMC,001712.037,V,,,,,,,150209,,,N*43
$GPVTG,,T,,M,,N,,K,N*2C
$GPGGA,001713.037,,,,,0,00,,,M,0.0,M,,0000*56
$GPGLL,,,,,001713.037,V,N*7A
$GPGSA,A,1,,,,,,,,,,,,,,,*1E
$GPRMC,001713.037,V,,,,,,,150209,,,N*42
$GPVTG,,T,,M,,N,,K,N*2C
$GPGGA,001714.037,,,,,0,00,,,M,0.0,M,,0000*51
$GPGLL,,,,,001714.037,V,N*7D
$GPGSA,A,1,,,,,,,,,,,,,,,*1E
$GPRMC,001714.037,V,,,,,,,150209,,,N*45
$GPVTG,,T,,M,,N,,K,N*2C
$GPGGA,001715.037,,,,,0,00,,,M,0.0,M,,0000*50
$GPGLL,,,,,001715.037,V,N*7C
$GPGSA,A,1,,,,,,,,,,,,,,,*1E
$GPGSV,1,1,00*79
$GPRMC,001715.037,V,,,,,,,150209,,,N*44
$GPVTG,,T,,M,,N,,K,N*2C
$GPGGA,001716.037,,,,,0,00,,,M,0.0,M,,0000*53
$GPGLL,,,,,001716.037,V,N*7F
$GPGSA,A,1,,,,,,,,,,,,,,,*1E
$GPRMC,001716.037,V
pi@raspberrypi
```

The device returns raw readings to you, which is a good sign. Unfortunately, there isn't much good data here, as the robot is indoors. How do you know this? Look at one of the lines that starts with $GPRMC; this line should tell you your current latitude and longitude values. The GPRS reports the following code:

```
$GPRMC,001714.037,V,,,,,,,150209,,,N*45
```

The preceding line of data should take the form shown in the following table, with each field separated by a comma:

0	1	2	3	4	5	6	7	8	9	10	11	12
$GPRMC	1714.037	V							150209		N	*45

The following table offers an explanation of each of the fields shown in the preceding table:

Field	Value	Explanation
1	220516	Timestamp
2	V	Validity: A (OK) and V (invalid)
3	Empty	The current latitude
4	Empty	North or South
5	Empty	The current longitude
6	Empty	East or West
7	Empty	The speed, in knots, at which you are moving
8	Empty	Course: The angular direction in which you are moving
9	150209	Date-stamp
10	Empty	Magnetic variation: The variation between magnetic and true North
11	N	East or West
12	*45	Checksum

In this case, the second value in the string is reporting V or that the unit cannot find enough satellites to get a position. Take the unit outdoors, and you can get the result shown in the following screenshot from your measgps.py program:

Note that the $GPRMC line now reads as follows:

```
$GPRMC,194827.000,A,4349.1418,N,11146.1046,W,0.00,,111213,,,A*64
```

Now the values will be as shown in the following table:

Field	Value	Explanation
1	020740.000	Timestamp
2	A	Validity: A (OK) and V (invalid)
3	4349.1426	The current latitude
4	N	North or South
5	11146.1064	The current longitude
6	W	East or West
7	1.82	Speed, in knots, at which you are moving
8	214.11	Course: The angular direction in which you are moving
9	021013	Date-stamp

10		Magnetic variation: The variation between magnetic and true North
11		East or West
12	*7B	Checksum

Now you have some indication of where you are; however, the GPS data is in raw form, which may not mean much. In the next section, you will figure out how to do something with these readings.

Accessing the USB GPS programmatically

Now that you can access the GPS device, let's work on accessing the data programmatically. Your project should now have the GPS device connected and have access to query the data via the serial port. In this section, you will create a program to use this data to discover where you are, then you can determine what to do with that information.

If you've completed the previous section, you should be able to receive the raw data from the GPS unit. Now you want to be able to do something with this data; for example, find your current location and altitude and then decide whether your target location is to the West, East, North, or South.

First, get the information from the raw data. As noted previously, the position and speed is in the $GPMRC output of the GPS device. Write a program to simply parse out a couple of pieces of information from that data. So, open a new file (you can name it location.py) and edit it, as shown in the following screenshot:

```python
#!/usr/bin/python
import serial
ser = serial.Serial('/dev/ttyUSB0', 4800, timeout = 1)
x = ser.read(1200)
pos1 = x.find("$GPRMC")
pos2 = x.find("\n", pos1)
loc = x[pos1:pos2]
data = loc.split(',')
if data(2) == 'V':
    print 'No location found'
else:
    print "Latitude = " + data[3] + data[4]
    print "Longitude = " + data[5] + data[6]
    print "Speed = " + data[7]
    print "Course = " + data[8]
```

The code lines are explained as follows:

- `#!/usr/bin/python`: As always, this line simply makes this file available for you to execute from the command line.
- `import serial`: You again import the `serial` library. This will allow you to interface the USB GPS sensor with the GPS system.
- `if __name__=="__main__":`: The main part of your program is then defined using this line.
- `ser = serial.Serial('/dev/ttyUSB0', 4800, timeout = 1)`: This command sets up the serial port to use the `/dev/ttyUSB0` device, which is your GPS sensor using a baud rate of `4800` and a timeout value of `1`.
- `x = ser.read(500)`: This command then reads a set of values from the USB port. In this case, you read 500 values, which includes a fairly complete set of your GPS data.
- `pos1 = x.find("$GPRMC")`: This will find the first occurrence of `$GPRMC` and set the value `pos1` to that position. In this case, you want to isolate the `$GPRMC` response line.
- `pos2 = x.find("\n", pos1)`: This will find the end of this string of text.
- `loc = x[pos1:pos2]`: The `loc` variable will now hold the path that includes all of the information you are interested in.
- `data = loc.split(',')`: This will break your comma-separated line into an array of values.
- `if data[2] == 'V':`: You now check to see whether or not the data is valid. If not, the next line simply prints out that you did not find a valid location.
- `else`: If the data is valid, the next few lines print out the various pieces of data.

The following screenshot is an example showing the result that appeared when my device was able to find its location:

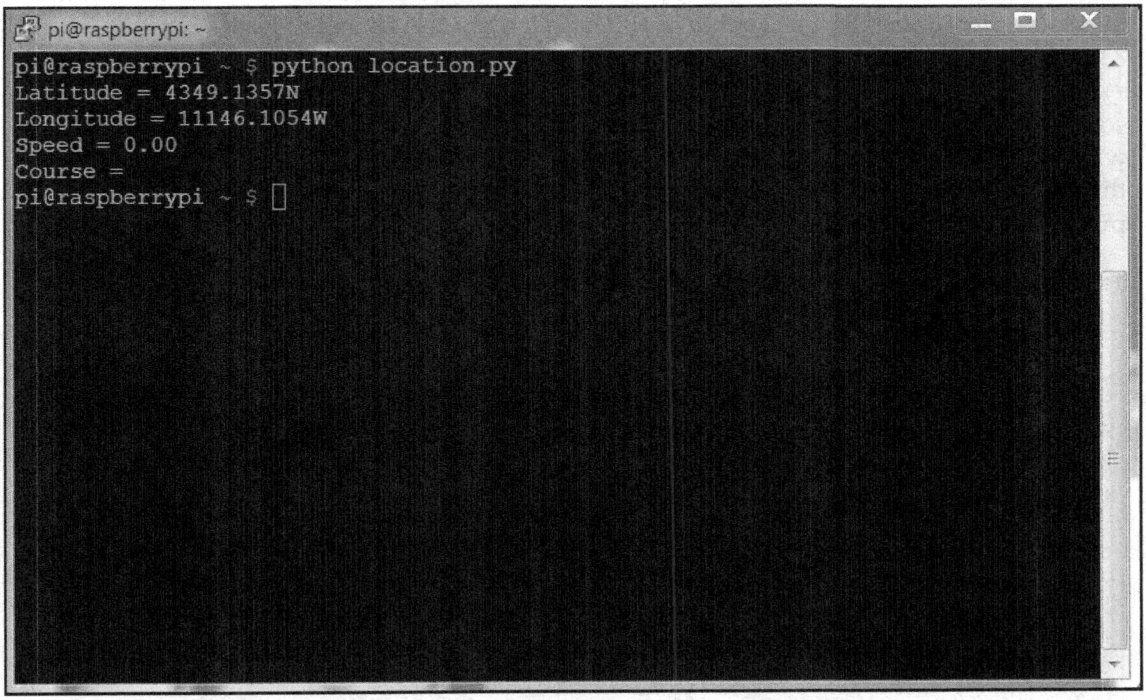

```
pi@raspberrypi: ~

pi@raspberrypi ~ $ python location.py
Latitude = 4349.1357N
Longitude = 11146.1054W
Speed = 0.00
Course =
pi@raspberrypi ~ $ 
```

Once you have the data, you can do some interesting things with it. For example, you may want to figure out the distance from and the direction to another waypoint. There is a piece of code at http://code.activestate.com/recipes/577594-GPS-distance-and-bearing-between-two-GPS-points/ that you can use to find the distances from and bearings to other waypoints, based on your current location. You can easily add this code to your location.py program to update your robot on the distances and bearings to other waypoints.

Now your quadcopter knows where it is and the direction it needs to go toward to get to other locations! There is another way to configure your GPS device that may make it a bit easier to access the data from other programs; it is using a set of functionality held in the `gpsd` library. To install this capability, type `sudo apt-get install gpsd gpsd-clients`, and this will install the `gpsd` software. For a tutorial on this software, go to `http://wiki.ros.org/gpsd_client/Tutorials/Getting%2Started%2with%2gpsd_client`. This software works by starting a background program (called a daemon) that communicates with your GPS device. You can then just query this program to get the GPS data. To start the process, type `sudo gpsd /dev/ttyUSB0 -F /var/run/gpsd.sock`. You can run the program by typing `cgps`.

The following screenshot shows a sample result:

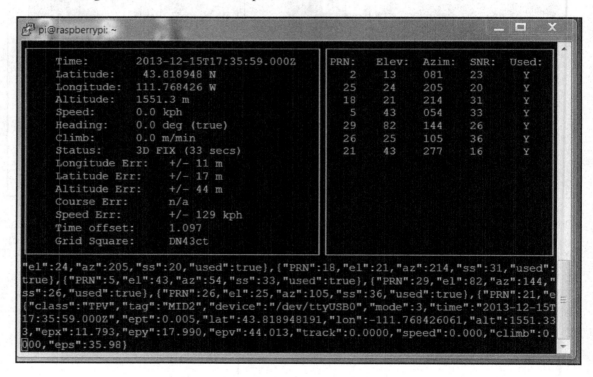

The preceding screenshot displays both the formatted and some of the raw data that is being received from the GPS sensor. If you get a timeout error when attempting to run this program, type `sudo killall gpsd` to kill all the running instances of the daemon and then type `sudo gpsd /dev/ttyUSB0 -F /var/run/gpsd.sock` again. You can also access this information from a program. To do this, edit a new file called `gpstry1.py`. The code will look like this:

```python
#!/usr/bin/python
import gps
session = gps.gps("localhost", "2947")
session.stream(gps.WATCH_ENABLE | gps.WATCH_NEWSTYLE)
while True:
    report = session.next()
    if report['class'] == 'TPV':
        if hasattr(report, 'time'):
            print report.time
```

The following are the details of your code:

- `#!/usr/bin/python`: As always, this line simply makes this file available for you to execute from the command line.
- `import gps`: In this case, you import the `gps` library. This will allow you to access the `gpsd` functionality.
- `session = gps.gps("localhost", "2947")`: This opens a communication path between the `gpsd` functionality and your program. It also opens port `2947`, which is assigned to the `gpsd` functionality, on the localhost.
- `session.stream(GPS.WATCH_ENABLE | GPS.WATCH_NEWSTYLE)`: This tells the system to look for new GPS data as it becomes available.
- `while True:`: This simply loops and processes information until you ask the system to stop (it can be stopped by pressing *Ctrl + C*).
- `report = session.next()`: When a report is ready, it is saved in the `report` variable.
- `if report['class'] == 'TPV':`: This line checks to see whether the report will give you the type of data that you need.
- `if hasattr(report, 'time'):`: This line makes sure that the report holds time data.
- `print report.time`: This prints the time data. I use this in my example because the time data is always returned even if the GPS is not able to see enough satellites to return the position data. To see other possible attributes, visit `http://www.catb.org/gpsd/gpsd_json.html` for details.

Once you have created the program, you can run it by typing `python gpstry1.py`. The following screenshot shows how the output should look after running the program:

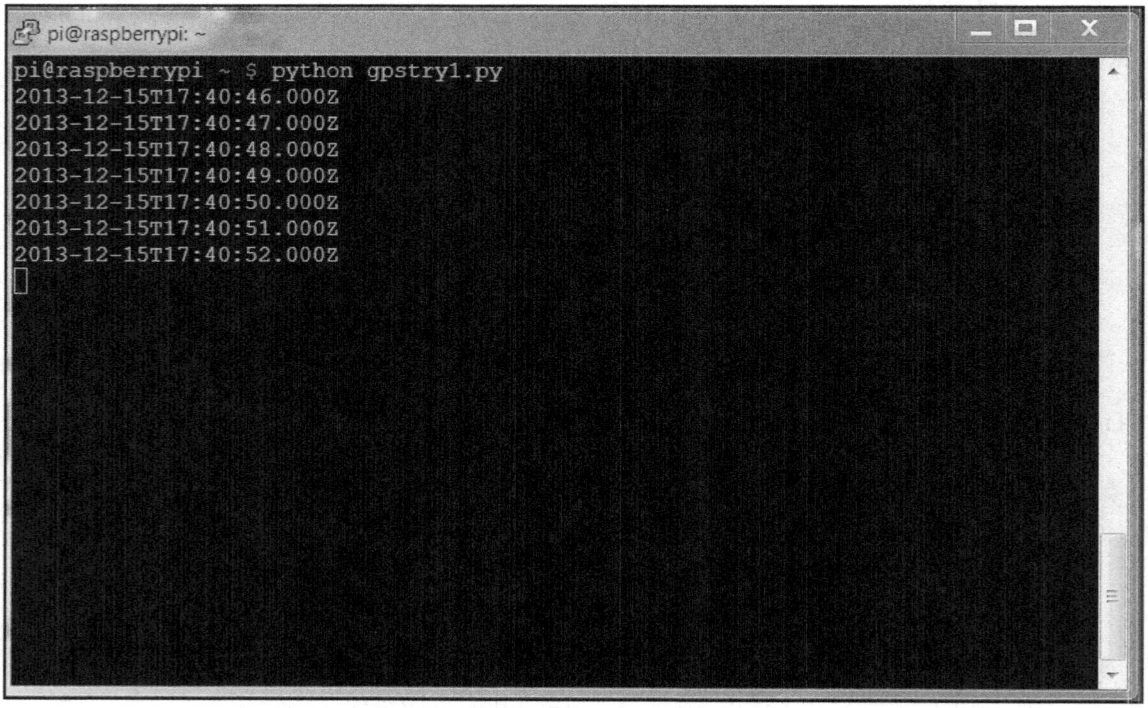

```
pi@raspberrypi: ~                                                    _  □  X
pi@raspberrypi ~ $ python gpstry1.py
2013-12-15T17:40:46.000Z
2013-12-15T17:40:47.000Z
2013-12-15T17:40:48.000Z
2013-12-15T17:40:49.000Z
2013-12-15T17:40:50.000Z
2013-12-15T17:40:51.000Z
2013-12-15T17:40:52.000Z
```

Now you have access to your position; you can use it for a number of different capabilities. Perhaps the most useful is planning your flight path. This information and the path-planning procedures are discussed at http://code.activestate.com/recipes/577594-GPS-distance-and-bearing-between-two-GPS-points/ in more detail. As a brief summary, if you know your current position and your desired future location, you can plan a path between the two. This will include an angle and a direction.

Summary

Now you have created a quadcopter that can fly itself or that you can control from a distance. You have also created a vast array of projects, and with a variety of capabilities, you're now ready to build your own robots and add new and unique capabilities. The sky is literally the limit now, as you plan new adventures in robotics using the Raspberry Pi!

Index

Measured Angle 188
MPU6050.py
  reference link 185

N

Nmap
  reference link 28

O

Open Source Computer Vision (OpenCV)
  about 153
  downloading 81, 84, 85
  installing 81, 84, 85
  reference links 87

P

PC
  and servo controller, communicating between
    117, 119
picamera
  reference link 144
PocketSphinx
  used, for accepting voice commands 65, 70, 71,
    72, 73
Pololu Maestro Servo Controller
  reference link 123
Pololu
  reference link 156, 160
program, in Linux
  creating, for controlling Wall-E robot's arms 122
Proportional-Integration-Derivative (PID) 188
Pulse-Width-Modulated (PWM) 113
PuTTY
  reference link 200
Python PID library code
  reference link 189
python-ardrone
  reference link 194
Python
  R2D2, controlling with Raspberry Pi 51, 55
  Raspberry Pi, used for controlling Wall-E robot's
    tracks 110

Q

quadcopter
  connecting, to hardware 194, 196
  GPS, adding 207
  hardware platform, accessing 194
  remote communications 197, 199

R

R2D2
  controlling remotely 86, 87
  controlling, with Raspberry Pi in Python 51, 55
  modifying 42
  motors, adding 43
  top, connecting to 48, 50, 51
  wheels, adding 43
Raspberry Pi 3
  about 6
  accessing, from host PC 14
  board, powering 8
  display, hooking up 9
  keyboard, hooking up 9
  mouse, hooking up 9
  operating system, installing 9, 10, 11, 12
  reference link 10
  setting up 6
Raspberry Pi Foundation
  reference link 10
Raspberry Pi Zero
  about 5
  board, powering 30
  display, hooking up 31
  Internet access, adding 35
  keyboard, hooking up 31
  mouse, hooking up 31
  operating system, installing 34
  setting up 29
Raspberry Pi
  about 5
  USB GPS, accessing programmatically 215
  used, for accessing Kinect 360 126, 129
  used, for controlling R2D2 in Python 51, 55
  used, for controlling servo controller 119, 120,
    121, 122
  used, for controlling Wall-E tracks in Python 110

CPSIA information can be obtained
at www.ICGtesting.com
Printed in the USA
FSOW03n1355301016
26771FS